West Michigan National Bank & Trust

The idea for *Images of Benzie County* originated with the Paul Oliver Memorial Hospital Auxiliary and West Michigan National Bank & Trust as a way of celebrating the heritage of Benzie County.

As we complete our fifteenth year of providing banking services in the community, we are convinced that Benzie County has embarked on a new era of progress. At West Michigan National Bank & Trust, we are proud of the role we have played and will continue to play in the years ahead.

Through words and pictures, this book shows an underlying dedication to a spirit of community in Benzie County through both times of adversity and times of prosperity. That legacy provides the framework for a bright future.

Robert C. Foster
President and Chief Executive Officer

Paul Oliver Memorial Hospital Illustration by Chris Patterson

IMAGES OF BENZIE COUNTY

BY THOMAS BEVIER

THE
DONNING COMPANY
PUBLISHERS

A lone loon on a placid lake, as shown in a print by nationally known Benzie County artist Gwen Frostic, is a familiar scene on the county's lakes. Frostic moved from the Detroit area to Benzonia forty-two years ago because the area was so rich in natural beauty. Courtesy of Gwen Frostic.

The Donning Company/Publishers
184 Business Park Drive, Suite 106
Virginia Beach, Virginia 23462

Steve Mull, General Manager
Debra Y. Quesnel, Project Director
Tracey Emmons-Schneider, Director of Research
Dawn V. Kofroth, Assistant General Manager
Elizabeth B. Bobbitt, Executive Editor
Paul C. Gualdoni Jr., Graphic Designer
Jim Casper, Imaging Artist
Teri S. Arnold, Senior Marketing Coordinator

Library of Congress Cataloging-in-Publication Data

BeVier, Thomas F.
    Images of Benzie County / by Thomas F. BeVier.
        p.   cm.
    Includes bibliographical references (p.   ) and index.
    ISBN 1-57864-024-5 (hardcover : alk. paper)
    1. Benzie County (Mich.)—History. 2. Benzie County (Mich.)—History—
Pictorial works. I. Title.
F572.B4B48   1998
977.4'32—dc21   97-46668
                                                     CIP

Printed in the United Sates of America

Contents

Foreword

Benzie County is the smallest in area and one of the least populated counties of Michigan's eighty-three, but in spite of that it has a fascinating history, which has been accurately researched and interestingly recorded by Mr. BeVier.

Other authors, nearly all of them local, have recorded bits of our history, but mainly in a highly localized manner, concentrating on various towns or neighborhoods, rather than the county as a whole.

Images of Benzie County provides a picture of the county from its first settlers to the present day in a verbal panorama that is both informative and interesting. It vividly portrays the county's economic vicissitudes and provides an interesting insight into the character of its people.

Reading Mr. BeVier's account brought back many memories. It is a well-organized chronology that should appeal to all who might have an interest in this beautiful part of Michigan.

His recounting of the events that are woven together to form this tapestry made me feel proud to have been a part of it for the past three-quarters of a century.

I have lived it and loved it and, through the reading of this book, I hope the reader will come to love it, too.

John W. Peterson

ACKNOWLEDGEMENTS

The Traverse Region, published in 1884, includes one of the earliest accounts of the way things were in Benzie County. Considering the youth of Michigan's smallest county at the time—it did not finally break away from Grand Traverse County until 1869—the anonymous author found that a surprisingly lot had already been written.

He admitted drawing heavily from writers who had gone before. "Many of the subjects herein treated have already been ably written upon . . .," he wrote. "Still others have discussed the varied resources for which this region is noted, but until now all these various interests have not been represented in one volume . . ."

The same unapologetic confession holds for *Images of Benzie County*, as well as the claim of providing continuity that previously has been lacking. That is not to minimize, however, the importance of the help and encouragement of a number of people. We will not attempt to list all of them, but we would be derelict in not mentioning several who played key roles.

Phyllis Foster deserves first mention. The book was her idea originally, and it was through her efforts that the Paul Oliver Memorial Hospital Auxiliary and West Michigan National Bank & Trust took on the project. She did much of the time-consuming work of gathering photographs and more than she probably realizes with her diplomatic suggestions that deadline was nigh.

The support of the bank was crucial. Kay E. Hommel, a past president of the auxiliary, spoke for all involved when she said, "We appreciate West Michigan National Bank & Trust for making this project possible. The proceeds will benefit the hospital."

Debbra Kerby, the manager of the Benzie Area Historical Museum, and the museum's Board of Trustees facilitated unhampered browsing through the documents and photographs which comprise the collection of one of the best historical society museums in Michigan. Librarians rarely get the credit they deserve for books like this. We are indebted to Cathy Carter at the Benzie Shores District Library, Jo Johnson at the Benzonia Public Library, and Julia McDonald at the Beulah Public Library.

The historical sketches Pete Sandman has written about Benzie County, ranging from the awakening to the economic significance of tourism with the building of the Royale Frontenac Hotel to details about the establishment of the peculiar pastime of soaring, were invaluable.

The book would not have been possible without the cooperation of many families who allowed the use of treasured photographs.

And to John W. Peterson, whose family owned the *Benzie County Patriot* (now the *Record Patriot*) from 1922 to 1972, we are beholden beyond measure. Not only did he graciously edit the manuscript, putting it in some sort of grammatical order, but he also provided insights which could only come from an involved, life-long resident. Any errors are, of course, the fault of yours truly.

Thomas BeVier

Gliders are a familiar sight in the Frankfort skies. The area was once one of the major soaring areas in the nation and for a short time had a glider manufacturing plant. Courtesy Benzie Area Historical Museum.

CHAPTER 1   SOARING: AN OVERVIEW

"We were isolated from the rest of the world, and the isolation was pleasant."

Bruce Catton (1899–1978),
Pulitzer Prize-winning author from Benzie County.

Harold Bruning has spent his adult life charting the geography of Benzie County, firstly as the county's official surveyor and secondly as a glider pilot. He knows it from the ground up, so to speak. It is safe to assume, then, that he understands as well as anybody the pleasant isolation Bruce Catton wrote about in *Waiting for the Morning Train,* a classic reminiscence of growing up in small-town America.

As luck would have it, Bruning was one of the pilots on duty on an early fall day when the Northwest Soaring Club was offering rides to the public at Frankfort City Airport to raise money to maintain the club's five gliders. Also on hand to fly the tow plane was Stollie Larson, who was a prime mover in reinvigorating the county's reputation as one of the best places in the nation for soaring.

"You get a good view of things from a glider," said Bruning, an active member of the club. "There isn't the distraction of engine noise you get in a small airplane. I think you'll be surprised at how quiet and peaceful it is. Soaring helps put things in perspective."

Bruning understands about looking at things from differing perspectives. He knows, for example, that a common way to look at any place is from the statistical viewpoint. But what does one really understand about Benzie County after learning that its 321.3 square miles make it the smallest of Michigan's eighty-three counties, that its estimated 1994 population was 13, 284 or that it has fifty-five inland lakes and two major rivers?

A description by Catton in his book, published in 1972—a description that still holds—is more instructive. It is a place, he wrote, "with fish to be caught and clear lakes for swimming, lonely streams for canoes and the big lake (Lake Michigan) itself for larger craft; here it is possible to escape from the steamy, overcrowded, overactive middle west and get back to something we knew long ago, when it was good enough just to breathe the clean air and feel sunlight and wind on your shoulders."

Pulitzer Prize-winning author Bruce Catton never forgot his Benzie County roots. Late in his life he returned and wrote *Waiting for the Morning Train*, a classic small-town reminiscence based on his growing up in Benzonia. Courtesy Benzie Area Historical Museum.

But even Catton, whose credentials included a 1953 Pulitzer Prize for a Civil War trilogy, sometimes had lapses. In writing about his hometown of Benzonia, he said that its "concerns were small—small enough to fit into the deepest recesses of the human heart—and its history was uneventful."

Provincial perhaps, but uneventful?

The stuff of the American ethic—hard work, resoluteness in the face of adversity, a strong sense of community—is anchored in quiet backwaters "removed from the current of change that swept down the mainstream," to borrow a Catton phrase. The relevancy of the history of Benzie County, and of other places similarly removed, lies not in singular cataclysmic events but in the accumulated weight of the thousand and one stories of people who never made a headline nor appeared on the nightly news.

Waiting for the Morning Train provides indirect corroboration of that proposition when the laureate of Benzie describes the small-town dramas of people he knew in his childhood. Their experiences obviously influenced his own course after he ventured into the larger world—taking the morning train from Beulah to Thompsonville and beyond to gain a national reputation as a journalist, historian, and author. One of the more poignant dramas involves his father, George R. Catton. He was the last headmaster of the Benzonia Academy and had the wrenching task of closing it in 1918, two years after Bruce was graduated. The institution had provided focus and purpose for fifty-five years in Benzonia, which was founded before the Civil War by idealistic Congregationalists. Originally, it was called Grand Traverse College and was the first institution of higher learning in the northwest Lower Peninsula of Michigan. It went through several permutations before finally becoming a high school academy.

The Mills Community House is the only one of the Benzonia Academy buildings remaining. It is now used as a community house and library by Benzonians. Photo by Thomas BeVier.

Still, there are those, and the suspicion is that Catton may have been one, who would minimize the significance of Benzie County's history because, for instance, the only presidential candidate ever to campaign there was William Jennings Bryan, in the early 1900s. As the founding and long-serving editor of *American Heritage* magazine in New York, Catton had perhaps become overly enamored with the so-called big historical events.

That is not to suggest, however, that he ever became disconnected from his small-town roots. He did, after all, return in his later years and purchase a home overlooking Crystal Lake on Glory Road, named after the title of one of his Civil War books by respectful local politicians. (Besides *Glory*, the trilogy included *Mr. Lincoln's Army* and *Stillness at Appomattox*.) Catton died in 1978.

One factor that he certainly didn't lose sight of in his writings was the importance of landscape in shaping history. Landscape and the effect it had on people's ideas and behavior provides the framework for *Morning Train*. It is as if the landscape were itself a character, a character for which he foresees a dire fate when he reflects on what people are doing to it: "And all the while, faster and faster, they consume or destroy the planet's own life sources—its growing things and its minerals, its soil and its air and its water—and the waste products arising from all of this lie upon the planet's flesh like an intolerable scurf."

Perhaps a glider ride would alleviate such pessimism.

The charms of soaring were brought to the area in the late 1920s when the Detroit Glider Council started coming up on weekends to ride the updrafts at the Sleeping Bear Dunes. Word of the ideal conditions spread, and in 1938 and 1939 the National Soaring Association held its annual soaring meets in Frankfort. In a fever of enthusiasm, local businessmen raised $15,000 to build the Frankfort Sailplane Manufacturing Co. and hired two well-known glider pilots, Stan Corcoran and Ted Bellak, to run it. There was talk, as the nation was preparing to enter World War II, that Frankfort would become the site for training military pilots. That did not materialize, and the glider plant was moved to Joliet, Illinois. After that there were only occasional flights until Larson and others organized the local soaring club in the 1970s.

Bruning was making a pre-flight inspection of a glider, one of several parked on the grass at the end of the airport runway.

"Climb in." he said. It was a tight fit for two under the Plexiglas bubble over the cockpit. "Stollie will tow us up to 6,000 feet and turn us loose." There was a slight jerk, and almost immediately the glider was dancing over the grass as the tow plane labored for takeoff at the other end of the rope. Then we were airborne. Minutes later we were above the Lake Michigan shore, and Bruning pulled a lever, releasing the glider from its tow.

Two gliders ride the updrafts near Lake Michigan. Courtesy Benzie Area Historical Museum.

The sun sparkled off Lake Michigan. Betsie Bay, postcard perfect with its marinas and the villages of Frankfort and Elberta on either side, were directly below. To the north, the steep faces of wind-crafted assertions of sand rose 400 feet and more from the shoreline, fulfilling their billing as the main attractions of Sleeping Bear Dunes National Lakeshore, which attracts nearly two million visitors a year. And in the distance, North and South Manitou Islands could be seen through the haze.

Bruning banked inland.

"Crystal Lake," he said nodding to the left. "Right there, at the east end, is where they cut the channel through to the Betsie River. It was a bad idea." (In 1873, an effort was made to link Crystal Lake to Lake Michigan by opening a channel. Since the water level of Crystal Lake was much higher than the big lake, the effort ended with a horrendous flood.)

Beyond Crystal Lake to the north, Bruning identified Long Lake, Platte Lake and Little Platte Lake. Upper Herring Lake and Lower Herring Lake lay to the south. He pointed out the Betsie River, surprisingly convoluted, and the Platte River, surprisingly wide. Benzie County is a reverie of water. And everywhere, in any direction you looked, there were trees. There were hints of towns—Honor, Thompsonville and maybe Lake Ann way off in the northeast corner of the county—but even Bruning could not be certain what lay under the canopy of green.

The trees—one of the life sources whose fate Catton so mourned—were all but removed from the landscape between 1860 and 1910. When he was growing up, much of Benzie County had been ravaged. Old photographs often show a welter of stumps and stacked logs, usually with lumberjacks standing around, smiling over their handiwork. The trees that so interfered with a view of the ground during the glider flight represent not only a great healing but also a change in public attitude.

"People today want to manage the forest for the long term," said Richard Cooper of Honor. Cooper, who has a degree in forestry from Michigan State University, has been advising people on how to do that for the last twenty years. He is probably more fascinated than most with northwest Michigan's early logging history, and he also knows better than most how short-sighted it was. "Back in those days, they didn't have any concern for the resource," he said. "With most of the people I deal with, looking out for the resource is their first priority."

The county has become a haven for nature artists and craftsmen.

"It's got everything I could want," said Gwen Frostic, whose drawings of birds, trees, and other natural wonders are known internationally. "It's got hills. It's got lakes. It's got dunes. It's the right spot for me."

Frostic, who is still active at ninety-one, ships prints and stationery to customers in every state and in many foreign countries. In the forty-two years she has had her studio in Benzonia, after leaving a job as a tool designer in the Detroit area to pursue her artistic career full-time, her business has grown from a single, hand-operated press to eighteen automated presses. But she is never too busy to personally autograph prints bought by the thousands of people who visit annually.

"From any angle you want to look at it, this has been the right spot for me," she said.

For good and ill, the lumbering era, more than any other, shaped the county's history, and for a long time the center would not hold. When trees were cut down in one place, loggers would move to another. The economic focus of the county shifted with each move. That phenomenon—and an abiding inability by the citizens of the various towns to work together—is reflected in fights over where the county offices were located. After starting out in Frankfort in 1870, the county seat was moved four times between 1870 and 1916.

Soaring is a family affair. Lawn chairs and picnic baskets are as much a part of a weekend gliding party as the actual flying.
Courtesy Benzie Area Historical Museum.

Sometimes gliders landed on the beach near Frankfort, as this one did in the 1940s. Courtesy Elvin Olsen Family.

It started out in Frankfort, but only after two referendums in which Benzonia came in second. Benzonians, however, did not give up. They formed an alliance with Homestead Township and won in another referendum in 1872. In 1873 the offices were moved to Homestead Road, near but not in Benzonia. The site was a mile from any accommodations, businesses, or a post office. Judges refused to hold court there, insisting on conducting proceedings in Case's Hall in Benzonia. "The present site (on Homestead Road) furnishes a striking illustration of the follies men are capable of when prompted by a spirit of jealousy and spite," wrote an observer at the time.

Nobody really wanted it there, so in 1891 the county trustees started looking for another location. Nine sites were nominated, including Crystal City (later to become Beulah), which was developing as a resort community, and Lake Ann and Thompsonville, which were thriving logging towns. It went back to Frankfort in 1894 where it remained until lumbering interests got it moved to Honor in 1908. Eight years later, however, with most of its neighboring forests gone and its future uncertain, the seat went to Beulah where it remained for sixty years in a former amusement and recreation center. It is still officially in Beulah, although only the natives know that for sure since the county offices were moved, in 1976, into a modern complex on U.S. 31 just down the hill from Benzonia. Old-timers like Bruning, the glider pilot, look back on that period with amusement, claiming that the hard-edged political animosities have been smoothed over. Well, at least almost.

"We're losing altitude," Bruning said. Updrafts were in short supply this day so the flight was briefer than it might have been. He turned toward the airport. The altimeter readings were foreboding to a novice soarer. Only a few hundred feet remained between the glider and ground zero.

But Bruning is used to ups and downs. It helps to be that way in Benzie County, and not only when flying gliders. In his seventy-seven years, he's seen the end of lumbering, the demise of the cross-lake railroad car ferry at Frankfort which was the economy's mainstay, and the emergence of a healthy tourism industry.

"Every flight is different, but things usually work out," he said, as the glider came to a smooth landing. Over the years, he had a few close calls, even coming down in Lake Michigan once. But he doesn't dwell on the past.

Bruce Catton, the master of historical flights of fact, would appreciate the sentiment.

"Pessimism has a fine tart flavor when you know everything is going to come out all right," he wrote toward the end of *Waiting for the Morning Train.*

Harold Bruning (left) and Stollie Larson, stalwarts in the Northwest Soaring Club, stand beside one of the club's five gliders. Photo by Thomas BeVier.

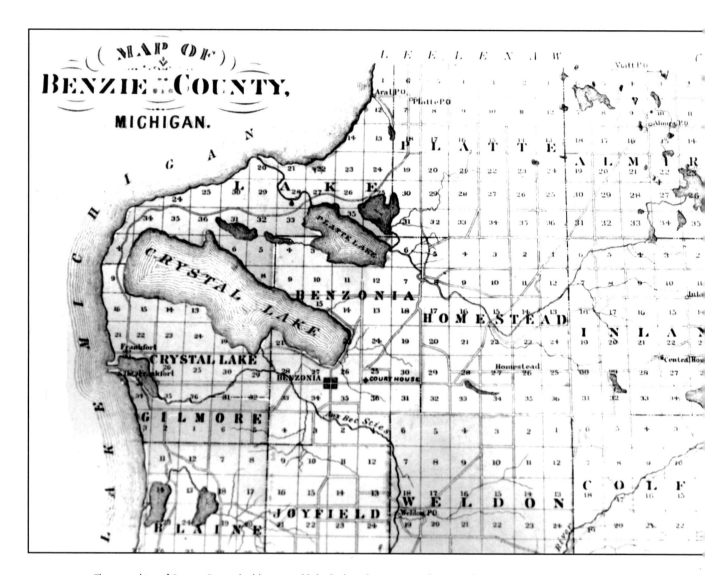

The townships of Benzie County had been established when this map was drawn in the 1880s.

CHAPTER 2 EARLY SETTLEMENT

They that dwell in the wilderness shall bow before him,
and his enemies shall lick the dust.

Psalms 72:9

In the pastoral middle of the nineteenth century, America offered a wilderness feast of near Biblical breadth: glorious forests and grasslands, rivers of uncharted currents and lakes of unplumbed depths, mountains high and valleys low. It was out there for the taking, west of the Ohio all the way to the Pacific. It had been previously taken from the Indians by a government that viewed untamed land as somehow tainted.

Where only moccasins had tread for centuries, the going was unforgiving and lonely, but there was no dearth of white settlers to take the dare: New England farmers weary of plowing rocky ground, immigrants honed for hardship by Europe's poverty, French Canadian loggers hungering for new forests to fell, and—as always in impassioned times—entrepreneurs and adventurers of various stripe and scheme. There were also, among the mix of motives, a few idealists whose ambition was not only to tame the wilderness, but also, under the strict rubrics of the New Covenant, to do some civilizing in the process. And so it was that a faithful few led by one Charles E. Bailey (1822–1894), a Congregational minister who, providentially perhaps, happened to have read a story from a New York newspaper extolling the charms and challenges of the Grand Traverse Region of Michigan, established Benzonia, the first settlement in what was to become Benzie County.

It was truly a pioneer venture.

"During the first few years of the existence of the colony, great inconvenience was experienced in consequence of the absence of roads," according to an early account of the harsh conditions. "All goods landed at Frankfort or brought from Glen Arbor (some thirty miles away on Sleeping Bear Bay to

The stoic Rev. Charles E. Bailey led the Congregational Colony's efforts to establish Benzonia in 1858. Later, he was also instrumental in the founding of Beulah on the shore of Crystal Lake.

the north in Leelanau County), where boats more frequently called, had to be transported in boats up the Betsie River, at no small cost of patience and labor. Up to 1862, there were no roads from Benzonia to other settlements. The mail route from Traverse City to Manistee by way of Benzonia was only a trail or footpath marked by blazed trees. In summer the mail was carried by horseback; in winter on a sort of sled, not unlike the dog sledges in use in some arctic countries."

They had another way of reaching the Benzonia location, but it was equally as trying.

"A small boat was constructed that two men could carry, which was conveyed over the ridge that separates Lake Michigan and Crystal Lake and launched on the latter. The vicinity of the purchase would then be reached from Glen Arbor by coasting along the shore of Lake Michigan to the portage over the ridge, crossing it and passing the small boat up Crystal Lake to its eastern extremity. Returning from one of these visits, they were compelled by stress of weather to remain over Sunday near Point Betsie lighthouse, when Mr. C. E. Bailey improved the opportunity to preach to a small audience in a fisherman's shanty . . . The sermon was the first ever preached in Benzie County."

The Rev. Bailey and a handful of others, including a brother, a couple of brothers-in-law and a fellow pastor, had explored first in Iowa and Missouri looking for a place to establish a religious community and a college far removed from urban temptations and modeled after the radical tenets of the temperance and abolitionist movements Bailey had embraced as a student at Oberlin College in Ohio. Then they visited the northwest corner of the Lower Peninsula of Michigan and there, on a hill overlooking the southeast shore of Crystal Lake, they found their site. They established a colony (the word they themselves used) in 1858 and called it Benzonia, a name taken from a Greek word meaning "good place to live."

The Grand Traverse Region, a history published in 1884 by H. R. Page & Co. of Chicago (from which the foregoing descriptions of early travel conditions were taken) credits the Benzonia Colony as being the first settlement, but other settlers had come before them. (Benzie County was not officially established until 1863 and from 1863 to 1869 it was a county in name only. During that period, Grand Traverse County governed it, as it also did Leelanau County. It was not until March 30, 1869, that the state legislature passed an act allowing the county to establish a government of its own. In the beginning, the Crystal Lake Township encompassed the entire county, but subsequently it was divided to include eleven others: Almira, Benzonia, Blaine, Colfax, Gilmore, Homestead, Inland, Joyfield, Lake, Platte, and Weldon.)

"In the spring of 1858, when the projectors of the colony arrived, there were a few white persons already living in the county," according to the Chicago publisher's history. "There was a man at the lighthouse (at Point Betsie on Lake Michigan), three families at the mouth of Betsie River, and a man named Averill had a sawmill at Herring Creek, Just how long these people had been in the county is not known and not important as the development of Benzie County began with the advent of the colony."

The Benzonia Colony was certainly the first formal settlement, and from its inception its political influence was pervasive; the name of the county, after all, is a contraction of Benzonia. The naming of places back then often involved such linguistic shenanigans. The Indians called the river "Un-Zig-A-Zee-Bee," which meant "River of the Sawbill (Merganser) Duck." From that, early French explorers made "Aux Bec Scies," which, to American sailors, sounded a lot like "Betsie." So "Betsie" it became for the river and for Betsie Bay, or, as it's sometimes called, "Betsie Lake."

In the 1860s, before the inlet to Betsie Bay was dredged, clapboard houses and fishing shanties overlooked the harbor entrance. The village of Frankfort was beginning to develop on the north shore. Courtesy Lois Bender.

The early history surely understates the importance of activity that was already going on around the mouth of the Betsie River before the establishment of the colony. Because overland travel was difficult in the 1850s—makeshift roads to Manistee to the south and to Traverse City to the north were not built until the early 1860s—the principal means of travel was by water. The harbor provided the most practical way to breach the forbidding isolation of the region.

For centuries before the first white settlers, the Indians, primarily the Ottawa and Chippewa, had hunted and trapped and fished around the lakes and rivers and along the Lake Michigan Shore northward from present-day Chicago to the Straits of Mackinac. They harvested wild berries, healing herbs, and barks. They grew crops—corn, beans, potatoes, and pumpkins—which they stored in pits below the frost line to eat through the winter. For the most part, the Indians left the land as they found it, accommodating themselves to its rigors rather than trying to change it. Their villages consisted of wooden frameworks covered with bark and animal skins. At one time, before curiosity seekers and developers destroyed them, there were five burial mounds at the mouth of the Betsie. They were all gone long before the turn of the century, as were most other traces of Indian culture. A state historical marker near the mouth of the Betsie on the north side of the bay beside a street now named Fr. Marquette Circle serves by implication as a poignant reminder of the former influence of the Indians. It reads:

"On May 18, 1675, Fr. Jacques Marquette, the great Jesuit missionary and explorer, died and was buried by two French companions somewhere along the Lake Michigan shore of the Lower Peninsula. Marquette had been returning to his mission at St. Ignace, which he had left in 1673 to go exploring in the Mississippi and Illinois country. The exact location of Marquette's death has long been a subject of controversy. Evidence presented in the 1960s indicates that this site, near the natural outlet of the Betsie River, at the northeast corner of a hill that was here until 1900, is the Marquette death site and that the Betsie is the Riviére du Pére Marquette of early French accounts and maps. Marquette's bones were reburied at St. Ignace in 1677."

It is unlikely Marquette would have succeeded in his heroic explorations if he had not had help from the Indians. If he was indeed originally buried at the mouth of the Betsie—a claim, which has been accepted by the Michigan Historical Society despite like claims by Ludington and Charlevoix—it was near the ancient Indian burial ground. His body was moved to St. Ignace out of affection for him on the part of the Indians. They thought it was a more fitting resting place because that was where he had established a mission in 1671. In an account of Marquette's death, Catherine L. Stebbins quotes from the writings of Marquette's superior in Quebec, Fr. Claude Dablon. "God . . . put it into their (the Indians) hearts to remove his bones and bring them to our church at the mission of St. Ignace . . ." he wrote, adding that there was a funeral procession of thirty canoes.

Sometime around 1850 (the exact year varies in historical accounts), Joseph Oliver, a trapper and fisherman who had served as a guide to government surveyors, built a cabin on the south side of Betsie Bay. He began rais-

The late Allen Blacklock, a former Elberta village president, wrote a definitive history of Betsie Bay. Allen Blacklock Collection.

ing a family with his Cree wife. He was later active in the formation of Gilmore Township. Their son, known as "Little Joe," was the first child of white ancestry born in what was to become Benzie County, and he became a Great Lakes boat captain. Other settlers soon joined them, including John Greenwood and Frank Martin. Martin's aversion to chilly winds, it was claimed, led to the naming of Frankfort. Several sources, including *Michigan Place Names* by Walter Romig, state that Frankfort got its name because the area reminded a German immigrant of the terrain around his hometown. But Allen B. Blacklock, who wrote a fine, comprehensive history of Elberta and the area around the harbor, argued convincingly that the name came about in a more whimsical way. Blacklock died in 1991 after serving for a number of years as president of the Village of Elberta. He wrote that descendants of Martin told him that while Martin was staying during the winter in Joe Oliver's cabin he and his friends built a makeshift log and brush barrier against the winds off Lake Michigan. Thereafter, it was jokingly referred to as Frank's Fort, and the name stuck, Blacklock wrote.

A lighthouse at Point Betsie, five miles north of the river's mouth, was built in the 1850s, and there were a number of commercial fishing operations along the shore. At first, only small boats entered the harbor because a sand bar at its entrace made for shallow draft. In 1854, however, a schooner on its way to Chicago was caught in a gale and, in panic, managed to gain refuge in the harbor. The captain was so impressed with the harbor's potential that he told the wealthy Buffalo, New York, owner of the shipping company for which he sailed, about it. The shipping company magnate, George W. Tifft, acquired most of the land around the harbor. He then sold it to George S. Frost of Detroit and other speculators, who established the Frankfort Land Co. in 1859. They set about lobbying Congress to appropriate money to improve the harbor, but the improvements had to wait until the end of the Civil War.

Originally, Frankfort included both the north and south sides of the harbor but later, as prideful differences developed between the settlements that faced each other across the lake, the south side broke away and called itself South Frankfort. South Frankfort dropped the Frankfort from its name in 1911, changing it to Elberta in recognition of the peaches grown in neighboring orchards. The woman who suggested the new name, in a contest among residents, was awarded a five-dollar cash prize and a box camera.

Benzonia was well established by the end of the Civil War. The Congregational Church, built in 1887, is still in use as the Benzie Area Historical Museum. The other buildings pictured here are now gone, as is the college founded by the colony. The Benzonia Academy closed in 1918. Courtesy Benzie Area Historical Museum.

With the exception of a few scattered farmers and loggers, development prior to the end of the Civil War in 1865 was mainly around present Frankfort and Benzonia. Benzonia, which had a strictly enforced ban of alcohol ("except for medicinal and mechanical purposes") and of tobacco and required observance of the Sabbath, was referred to as Piety Hill by outsiders who considered its world view from its location overlooking Crystal Lake as sanctimonious. Even some people who lived in Benzonia found the bans cloying, especially because being found guilty of violation could result in forfeiture of land. ("For the sake of the reputation of some members of the colony, it is to be hoped that the contention growing out of this subject will forever remain an unwritten history," an early commentator wrote.) Frankfort was a more rumble-tumble place where fishermen, loggers, and sailors behaved as fishermen, loggers, and sailors often do.

The sober discipline of the Benzonians may account for their attention to record keeping, which noted every tithe and land title and—to the advantage of this chronicle—a good deal about the ventures and adventures of Bailey. He certainly was not the typical settler or the typical preacher either, for that matter, but then it would be difficult to describe a typical settler, given the diversity of individuals who prevailed. It does not seem an exaggeration to suggest that Bailey's personality traits point up the sort of stuff it took—dogged determination being not the least of it—to make a place in the hinterland. Minister or not, he shared all the common hardships. A cleric back then was "not afraid to take off the broadcloth and put on the denim," as the late Leonard L. Case, whose family was among early Benzonia settlers and is still prominent in the area, observed in a history he wrote. Or, he might have added, also not averse to taking advantages of opportunities in business and land speculation.

Bailey was born in Westmoreland, New York, on July 1, 1822, the son of a farmer and broom manufacturer. He attended several colleges, most significantly Oberlin, in northern Ohio. The influence of Oberlin, which was one of the few schools in the country that was co-educational and admitted blacks, is apparent in the mission statement of the college the colony established in Benzonia: "To afford to both sexes, without distinction of color, the opportunity of acquiring a liberal education." (It perhaps begs the question to observe that no blacks joined in the settlement.) Rev. Bailey was a minister in Medina, Ohio, in 1855 when he conceived the idea of founding a Christian colony and college. He persuaded several others to join in the endeavor.

A decade after Congregationalists settled Benzonia in 1858, businesses lined the Main Street as neatly as pews in a church. There was a three-story school within walking distance of home for every child in town. Courtesy Benzie Area Historical Museum.

Frankfort had become a respectable-sized town by the 1880s, although with its dirt
streets and paint-bare clapboard buildings it was a bit more earthy than was
portrayed in an artist's rendering in an early history of the Grand Traverse Region.
Photographs Courtesy of the Charles Webb Fairchild Family and James Thorpe.

He was a tall man with the reputation as an excellent horseman. A beard framed his severe visage. He did not have a mustache. In recollections of early settlers published by the Michigan Pioneer and Historical Society in 1904, there are anecdotes about him that have become a part of Benzie County folklore. For instance, there was the accident that occurred as he was boarding a boat in Chicago to bring his family north.

"The boat (the steamer *Galena*) starting a little before her time found Mr. Bailey and family on the swing bridge and the bridge was open," according to the account. "He hailed the captain, who stopped at a dock lower down outside of three other boats. Hurrying across with a heavy satchel in each hand in the darkness Mr. Bailey stepped into an open hatch and fell to the bottom of the hold striking on a heap of stove coal, which could have killed him if the stachels had not been under him; although seriously injured he succeeded in getting up and assisted his family to the boat and then sank away helpless. After reaching Glen Arbor it was decided to look farther, and the party shouldered their knapsacks and with the section lines and their compass for their guide they traveled through the forest (Mr. Bailey being obliged to walk with two canes)."

On another occasion, he became impatient on a boat while he was on his way to the state capital in Lansing for a land sale. "The wind was light and contrary, so he persuaded the captain to run as near land as he dared, when Mr. Bailey jumped overboard and swam ashore, and making the best use of his strength and time, he reached Lansing in season."

His influence dominated. He was the pastor of the Benzonia Congregational Church when it was founded in 1860 and secretary of Grand Traverse College when it was organized in 1863. He was the first postmaster, proprietor of the first general store and a land agent. His great granddaughter, Dorothy B. Hensel, who detailed his influence when she wrote *Church of the Wilderness,* a history of the First Congregational Church in Benzonia, said in an interview that he sometimes rankled other church members.

"The fathers of the church said he was doing too many things, and that he should do more to take care of the parishioners," she said. "He told them they should take care of themselves. That about sums up his personality."

(In the early 1880s, Bailey resigned his positions with the church and the college and moved with his family to Maryland. He returned in 1886 for the funeral of his brother Lorenzo and moved back permanently in 1887. He died of a heart attack, at the age of 72, on May 16, 1894.)

The membership of the First Congregational Church of Benzonia, which included nearly everybody in town, grew from eighteen at its inception to several score within two years and to one hundred and forty in 1872, as new believers arrived. In the early years, the congregation met in several locations, including, at one point, sharing a church with Methodists. It was not until the 1880s that the membership decided it was time to build a church, and in 1887 the first services were held in a handsome church of Gothic Revival architecture. The building served as a church until 1968 when a new, modern church was dedicated. According to the original deed, if the old church property ceased being used for religious purposes, it reverted to the heirs of C. E. Bailey on whose land it was built. Mrs. Hensel, his last living heir, promptly gave it to the Benzie Area Historical Society, and it now houses one of the finest regional museums in the state.

Grand Traverse College also began in a makeshift way, with thirteen students meeting for classes in the kitchen of the widow of a soldier who had been killed in the Civil War. Each settler who purchased government land was required to give a quarter of his holdings to the college with the idea (unrealistic, as it turned out) that proceeds from future sales would serve as an endowment for the school. The first college building, a log classroom, was opened in 1867. A chapel was dedicated in 1869.

The Benzonia Concert Band, made up of students and faculty of the college, played a major role in the cultural life of the community. Norman Covey Collection.

The college was the first institution of higher learning in northwest Michigan, and for decades it provided teachers for the region's schools. From its inception, it never overcame the problems of lack of funds and isolation. It struggled for fifty-five years. It changed its name to Benzonia College and then to Benzonia Academy as it struggled for a niche. When it closed in 1918, it had three substantial buildings: Barber Hall, with classrooms, a library, laboratory and assembly room; Bailey Cottage, the boys dormitory; and Mills Cottage, which provided housing for the school's principal and served as the girls dormitory and the school's dining room. Only one, the handsome, three-story brick Mills building, remains. It has served as Benzonia's community center and library since 1925.

While Bailey and his kith and kin were beginning to fulfill their energetic vision during the Civil War, Frankfort languished, but that was soon to change. When the war ended, the nation's attention turned to development in the interior. In 1866 Congress appropriated $98,000 for harbor improvement and work began the following year. The channel was dredged to allow vessels with a ten-foot draft to enter the harbor from Lake Michigan. Two piers, each eight hundred feet in length, were constructed on the north and south sides, along with a new lighthouse. The results were immediate and dramatic.

With the opening of Betsie Bay as a harbor for large ships, it became a favorite for the two-masted schooners, which carried lumber and other freight throughout the Great Lakes. Courtesy Benzie Area Historical Museum.

By the turn of the century, the handsome two-masted schooners that had been so much a part of the development of cities around the Great Lakes were being replaced by steam-powered vessels. One of the last of the sailing ships, its sails in tatters, is shown leaving the Frankfort Harbor. Courtesy Congregational Summer Assembly.

Wood-hauling schooners by the score, which had avoided Frankfort before, transformed the deep-water harbor into a pageantry of sails. Steam-powered vessels, which after the turn of the century would largely replace the sailing ships, also made it a regular stop to take advantage of the lively commerce that was developing. The early steamers also brought passengers and with them the rudiments of the area's tourism industry.

Where in 1866 there had been half a dozen families living on Betsie Bay, by 1869 the population was around five hundred. There were several sawmills. Plans to build the Frankfort Iron Works were in the offing to take advantage of the large hardwood stands in the area. The trees were used to make charcoal to use as fuel in smelting ore brought in from the Upper Peninsula. The Iron Works was the county's first major industry. It operated

The building of a new pier with a lighthouse at the end marked the way into Betsie Bay for the largest steamboats on the Great Lakes. Broad-beamed barges brought in stone to build a new pier in a huge harbor improvement project. For the local citizenry it was the best show in town. Courtesy Charles Webb Fairchild Family and M. E. Palmer.

The Frankfort Iron Works, which operated from 1870 to 1883 in South Frankfort (later Elberta), was the first major industry in Benzie County. The stacks of cordwood in the foreground are an indication of the tremendous amount of hardwood it took to fuel the plant. Courtesy Benzie Shores District Library.

The south side view of the Frankfort Iron Works shows the stack of the furnace that was used to smelt ore. The inclined track on the left carried charcoal to the furnace. Courtesy Benzie Shores District Library.

from 1870 to 1883, when it closed because it had exhausted its fuel supply. While it lasted, men worked twelve-hour shifts to keep it going. There were ten brick kilns for making charcoal.

The economic activity spawned other businesses. There were three hotels, eight stores, a blacksmith, a gunsmith, a tinsmith, a dentist, a doctor and—of course—a lawyer. It also was noted, in an 1871 report of the phenomenal changes occurring on Betsie Bay, that Frankfort had at long last gotten religion, with forty-five Congregationalists, twenty Methodists, and twelve Baptists being accounted for at religious services.

Benzie County has historically had few African Americans residents. The Baty family of Joyfield was an exception and, judging from their stylish wardrobe in this picture taken in 1914, they apparently prospered. Courtesy Benzie Area Historical Museum.

Every town had its own baseball team and rivalries were intense. Shown here is the Joyfield Baseball team in 1915. Courtesy the Joy Family.

During the latter 1860s and the 1870s, Frankfort and Benzonia developed in concert but in distinctive ways. A single newspaper, for instance, could not serve both communities. In 1870 both got their own paper, first The Benzonian and shortly thereafter The Frankfort Express. The early wariness persists to the present day, albeit with most of the sharp edges rounded off.

Beginning in the 1870s with a logging boom made possible by Frankfort harbor improvements and the advent of the railroads, other communities would move onto center stage and Benzie County would become a much fuller place.

CHAPTER 3 THE LOGGING ERA

"This was the last of them (logging camps). Louie Sands was the last . . .
That was a big operation, and he finished up in there and
after that it developed into this smaller deal."

Ellsworth Emmett Joy (1895–1977), who was there in 1912

When Louie Sanderson came to Benzie County from Sweden in the late 1800s, so the story goes, the first thing he did was whittle down his name to Sands to make it more American sounding. The second thing he did was to begin cutting down trees.

He started only with what a lot of new settlers had—forty acres, a couple of oxen and not much more. But when one of his team died, rather than rail against his luck, as lesser men might have done, he put his own neck in the yoke and kept on hauling logs. When he ran out of trees to fell on his homestead, he bought more timberland and then more and more until he owned seven full sections near Thompsonville. He got rich eventually and bought a limousine. But, as Ellsworth Joy recalled in *Daylight in the Swamp*, an oral history of logging in northern Michigan by William and Edith Overlease, success didn't change Sands.

"He never outlived his old lumberjack days," Joy said. "He used to like to come and eat in the lumber camp."

Nevertheless, the heedless cutting of the virgin forest took place with little thought to the fact that it was a limited resource. No matter how lush and never-ending it appeared in the beginning, the excesses of the early lumber barons led to the inevitable end to an industry that played a profound role in northern Michigan's development.

The Betsie River was a flood of logs during the area's lumber boom. Here loggers ("river rats," they were called in the vernacular of the time) take a rare break, leaning on their peaveys as they pose for a photographer. Courtesy Benzie Shores District Library.

Toward the end of his life, Joy revisited the site of what he remembered as the last of the large lumber camps. The only evidence he found of its existence was an antique whisky bottle and a special hammer that had been used to knock snowballs out of horses' hooves.

The lumber boom in northern Michigan began shortly after the arrival of the first white settlers and proceeded apace until it began to wane around 1910. It shaped the lives of people like Joy who lived through it, even as it shaped the geography, the politics, and the economy of the region in ways that are still apparent. For instance, three of Benzie County's seven towns (Honor, Thompsonville, and Lake Ann) owe their very existence to lumbering and the other four (Frankfort, Elberta, Benzonia, and Beulah) are more than a little beholden.

Benzie County was, of course, part of a much broader phenomenon in the upper two-thirds of the state's Lower Peninsula and virtually all of the Upper Peninsula. But, as is pointed out by Overlease, what happened in Benzie County was universal, noting the "the lives of people working, living, dying in their own set of environmental and cultural limitations, has application and meaning to all men, everywhere."

Even though the recollections of the old-timers in the Overleases' book are softened by nostalgia, it is the hardships they witnessed and experienced that inform their stories, suggesting conditions that, by modern standards, would be unacceptable. Work started at dawn and proceeded till dark. The workers were for the most part young and uneducated and were sometimes cheated on their wages. If a man was injured or killed, as frequently happened, there was no private insurance or government program to help his or his family; fellow loggers took up a collection, tossing what few coins they could spare into a hat, and that was it. Housing for the workers was makeshift and drafty and the meanest and strongest ruled and got the best bunks. Often, there were no bathing facilities, and the high point of many of their workdays began and ended with all the buckwheat pancakes and syrup they could eat at breakfast.

By modern-day standards, life in the lumber camps was dismally spartan and the hours of work unbearably long. The camp pictured here on Crystal Lake was considered a cut above most others in creature comforts. Courtesy the Joy Family.

The loggers provide glimpses of what it was really like, and sometimes it was not pretty.

"Your bunks, they built along the wall . . ." said Jacob (Jake) Long (1872–1966), who was interviewed during the last year of his life. "You'd throw in an armful of hay in it and spread a blanket over it . . . you'd have two blankets. If you wanted a pillow, you'd put your pants or your coat, or mackinaw or whatever you had under your head. That was your pillow.

"Well, by god, I'll tell you, men lived healthy . . . and oh, gee yes, you wouldn't be healthy unless you had bedbugs and lice. That's what made you healthy . . . I've known men . . . I used to try to if I could . . . lots of 'em used to try, if they was where they could get their washin' done, they'd change clothes every week. They wouldn't get so lousy. Other men would go buy a suit of underclothes and put 'em on and keep 'em on all winter. In the spring when they'd go out of camp, they'd throw 'em away and get new."

With a verbal shake of the head, he recalled the work:

"You could figure on workin' til right around seven or eight o'clock. I don't know how in the world you ever stood the work . . . and put the hours in. Christ, pull out at four o'clock in the morning right here in the wintertime . . . getting daylight around seven o'clock . . ."

Still, whatever hardships the old-timers endured, the pride in workmanship shows throughout their comments, and, indisputably, they did get the job done.

In an interview, Overlease, a professor emeritus of West Chester University in Pennsylvania and a long-time summer vacationer in the Frankfort area, said Benzie County differed somewhat from many other locales in that most of the virgin timber was hardwood and that only about 10 percent was white pine. He said most of the prized pine grew along the Lake Michigan shore and in scattered stands elsewhere in the county. "It was the first to go," he said. The pine was in especially high demand after the great Chicago fire of October, 1871, which killed two hundred and fifty people and whose windblown sparks ignited fires on more than a million acres of timberland in lower Michigan and Wisconsin.

Loggers took the most easily obtainable timber first, and then took the rest of it, shipping it by two-masted schooners and Great Lakes steamboats on Lake Michigan. An 1870 picture of Frankfort provides a graphic portrayal as to the extent of early logging; there's barely a tree to be seen.

"That's our house," said Lou Wichert, who, with her husband, Edwin, has restored the very same house shown in the center of the picture to its original Victorian condition and turned it into the Frankfort Land Co.

Bed & Breakfast Inn on Leelanau Avenue. "There was a great view back then, but it must have been chilly with no trees to block the winds off the lake," she said.

The once-forested shores of Betsie Bay had been shorn of virtually all its trees by 1870. The house in the foreground was built on speculation by the Frankfort Land Co. That same house is today the oldest residence in Frankfort. It is a bed and breakfast operated by Lou and Edwin Wichert. Courtesy Al Hyames.

She believes the two-story Italianate house with a widow's walk on top, which was placed on the National Register of Historic Homes in 1995, was built on speculation by the Frankfort Land Co. several years after the company was founded in 1859. The Wicherts, who bought it in 1987, have provided the only extensive remodeling that had been done since it was built in 1872. The house was probably first used by officials of the land company as a place to stay when they visited Frankfort. It is the only remaining building constructed by the company.

Logging was underway before the Civil War. The first major operation in the county probably was a water-powered sawmill operated from 1851 to 1863 by Harrison Averill near the mouth of Herring Creek. Averill was his own man, and he lived by his own rules. Indeed, before fleeing the law himself—the government claimed he was cutting down trees that weren't his—he administered some frontier justice. In June 1854, a man who was traveling along the Lake Michigan shore in a small sailboat with his two children moored near Averill's mill while they trudged to Manistee to get supplies. When they returned, the boat was gone. Some time later, another man stopped at the mill with the boat. A trial was held on the spot. The culprit was tarred and feathered, soundly beaten, and sent on his way.

The demise of Averill's operation came as new logging technology was being developed. The Big Wheel, manufactured in nearby Manistee, allowed loggers to work more effectively in the summer, when the ground was wet and soft. One end of a stack of logs would be suspended on the axle of the fifteen-foot diameter wheels so they could be dragged more easily. The saws and engines in the mills were also greatly improved, although the major part of the work in the woods still depended mainly on the brawn of the men who swung the axes and paired on crosscut saws.

A boom mentality was pervasive. "Many chances are yet open, and money is waiting to roll into the pockets of some more who get there quick," one journalist wrote upon visiting Lake Ann. He also assured his readers that "there are no idlers here, no drones" and that "the people of the little burg are wide awake and energetic." And, "By the way," he added, "the fishing is extraordinary," citing the catch of a fourteen-pound pickerel and a six-and-a-half pound bass.

Logging operations and mills almost beyond counting cropped up here and there throughout the county. They were built along the Betsie and Platte Rivers, on the shores of many lakes and near any road or trail that held any hope for transporting the timber. Many of the early operations were one- or two-man affairs and frequently a farm family would get into logging to earn a few precious dollars to supplement the meager income that subsistence agriculture provided.

There were several steam-powered mills around Frankfort and South Frankfort (present-day Elberta), Benzonia and Beulah and backwoods operations in the county's interior. Fire was often the final chapter for a mill. One of the more spectacular fires was the one in 1909 that destroyed the A. G. Butler Mill, built in 1882 on the present site of Mineral Springs Park on the Frankfort waterfront.

The old loggers' boardinghouse in Watervale is now the hotel and restaurant of a resort on Lower Herring Lake that has been operated by the same family since 1917. A number of other buildings from the lumbering days also have been part of the resort operation. It has been modernized, but not so much as to lose the sense of an earlier, less hectic time. Photo by Thomas BeVier.

Only broken foundations, if that, remain of most of the early logging and sawmill operations. For the most part they are but dim memories in the minds of old-timers who remember when men were working in the woods from dawn to dark at almost forgotten occupations. Besides sawyers and teamsters, there were swampers cutting limbs off logs, road monkeys maintaining the logging roads and scalers tallying the day's production.

One sawmill town in the county remains nearly intact, with many of its original, clapboard buildings, It is Watervale, on the south end of Lower Herring Lake. It was built around 1890 and operated only until 1893, when it went bankrupt during a national financial panic. Besides a sawmill, with a daily capacity of 50,000 board feet of hardwood and 60,000 board feet of hemlock, the site had housing for workers and their families, including a large boarding house and a general store (called a casino). A railroad ran along the shoreline in front of the community, and there was a channel from Lower Herring Lake to Lake Michigan where there were piers for schooners to dock. After the mill closed, the site was purchased in its entirety by a Chicago ophthalmologist, Dr. Oscar Kraft, who first used it as a secluded vacation spot for his family. In 1917 it was turned into a resort. The original boarding house is now an eighteen-room hotel. There are twelve cottages (ten of them original) and the store building is used for parties and other gatherings. The resort has been owned by Kraft's descendants ever since. His great niece, Dori Turner, who took over for her elderly mother, Vera Kraft Noble, is now in charge. The resort does not advertise, depending on word-of-mouth and the allegiance of families who have been coming for generations.

"We've added modern conveniences, but we try to keep it as much like it was originally as practical," Turner said. "It became the place of my mother's heart."

Other communities suffered for lack of such affection. Three ghost towns in the county attest to that. Griner Station, in Colfax Township in the southeast corner of the county, was established in 1875 when John Griner built an inn, halfway between Benzonia and Traverse City. It died in 1889 when the Manistee & Northeastern Railroad was built and missed it by a mile. A Manistee lumberman, John O. Nessen, saw his opportunity and built Nessen City on the railroad line not far away. Nessen City had a hotel, the Northern, a general store and other businesses. There was logging nearby, with emphasis on rock elm that was shipped to a Cincinnati manufacturer of hames, the curved wooden pieces to which traces to a team of horses are attached.

The railroads opened the interior of the Grand Traverse Region for settlement. The Manistee & Northeastern was particularly important to Benzie County's early development.

Station and Nessen City are all but forgotten, but the third ghost town, Aral in Lake Township near the mouth of Otter Creek in the northwest corner of the county, lives on in local lore. It was the location of "murder most foul," as journalists of the time—the summer of 1889—were wont to say.

Aral had its beginning in 1880 when Daniel C. Thomas, who was returning from the California Gold Rush, purchased five acres just south of the Leelanau County line. He sold out shortly thereafter to Dr. Arthur O'Leary, a phrenologist who had made a name for himself on the national lecture circuit. O'Leary hired Charles T. Wright, who had previously managed a sawmill in Racine, Wisconsin. The sawmill went into operation in 1881 or 1882 and employed one hundred and fifty men, including fifty Ottawa Indians. It was officially named Aral in 1883 after a mill employee's home village in Ireland. O'Leary sold his interest to Wright.

Wright was over six feet tall and had a volatile temper. In *The Story of Aral,* written in 1989 by Theodore and Bonita Reuschel for the Benzie County Historical Society, Wright was described as having been raised in Arizona "to think that the gun was law." He was armed with a Marlin rifle and a revolver when a deputy sheriff, Neil A. Marshall, and a friend, Dr. Frank Thurber, showed up to serve a tax lien on a load of logs. Witnesses at a subsequent trial said there was an argument and struggle that ended with Marshall dead from a rifle shot to the heart and Thurber dead from pistol shots to the head and chest.

Reports of the details of what happened vary, but a hand-written account by Herman Bayne, Aral's postmaster and a bookkeeper at the mill, smacks of accuracy. According to Bayne, Wright "was a man who took a drink and then went about his business, but he was driven to desperation by the injustice (the tax lien) done him. He had happened to tip the bottle a little higher than ususal (the day of the killings), however, he was still able to navigate." After the shooting, Bayne wrote, Wright paid his employees their wages, ate supper, and then took to the woods. A hastily assembled posse, which included relatives of the shooting victims, soon followed. An unfortunate victim of the chase was an Indian youth who either refused to tell or did not know where Wright had gone. Posse members tied a rope around his neck, threw the end over a pine limb. "The poor fellow had a stiff, crooked neck the rest of his life," Bayne reported. As the Indian was being raised for the third time, he either told where Wright was hiding or Wright walked out of the woods on his own volition and surrendered, depending on which of several accounts is accurate.

Wright was later sentenced to life in prison, but in 1900, in one of his last official acts in office, Governor Hazen S. Pingree commuted the sentence to seventeen years and paroled him. "Pingree's name and fame were badly sullied in Benzie County long before his gargantuan statue was sullied by the over-fed pigeons in one of Detroit's downtown parks," Benzie County historian Leonard L. Case wrote.

Bayne was more sanguine. "While Wright has a right to go armed on his own premises in those days, it went against him to use those arms to shoot officers of the law," he wrote. "I felt for Thurber's and Marshall's families, and I felt for C. T. Wright and his wife. I also felt for the young Indian lad that had to go through life with a stiff, crooked neck."

After the shootings, Aral faded. For a time, the mill was operated by a religious sect, the Israelite House of David, whose members were known for their long hair and beards and their baseball prowess. By 1911 the lumber had run out. The last residents, the Bancrofts, were seen leaving in a Model T Ford in 1922. Evidence of the once lusty town has been steadily erased since it became a part of the Sleeping Bear Dunes National Lakeshore in 1970.

Thompsonville was once the center of commerce in Benzie County. Two railroads intersected there, and there was enough traffic to support several hotels. The Diamond Hotel was one of the finest north of Grand Rapids. Dinner was served family style at long tables. Courtesy Benzie Area Historical Museum.

The three lumber towns that survive—Honor, Thompsonville, and Lake Ann—beat the odds partly because of a growing tourism and outdoor recreation industry, but also because of an unyielding will. As John W. Peterson, former editor of the Frankfort *Patriot* (now the *Record Patriot*) observed, "There's nothing more stubborn at clinging to life than a small town."

Historical sketches of the three that have managed to hang on follow.

Thompsonville

Before cardboard and before plastic, merchandise was packed in wooden boxes. To supply the demand required vast stands of hardwood, and Benzie County had lots of it. So the area attracted a Massachusetts lumberman named Sumner S. Thompson, and fellow investors, including heirs of the Rev. Henry Ward Beecher, the famous nineteenth century preacher and writer. The town on the southern border of the county was named after Thompson when it was platted in 1890.

Thompson's mill, the Piqua Handle Co., made butter bowls and other containers and handles for everything from lawn mowers to umbrellas. There also was the Thompsonville Cooperage Co., which made, among other items, jointed wooden poles for World War I pup tents. Later, north of town at a place called Carter's Siding where Carter's Creek crosses Highway 669, the Desmond Chemical Co. used hardwood to produce charcoal, alcohol, acetates, and other wood derivatives that were in demand during World War I.

By the turn of the century, the population had soared to around 1,500, and Thompsonville was a sort of metropolis in the wilderness. There were two railroads, which went under several names before eventually becoming part of the east-west Ann Arbor and the north-south Pere Marquette, running through it on which to ship freight to Chicago, Detroit, and Grand

Rapids markets. Each railroad also had a passenger depot. Thompsonville's location at the intersection of secondary roads several miles from main highways is considered a liability today, but in the days of the railroads it didn't matter much as long as the trains stopped. There were two hotels, including the Diamond House, complete with a Chinese laundry. The hotel, which in its heyday was considered one of the finest in northern Michigan, burned in 1928. There were churches and schools, shops of various sorts, and a disproportionate number of saloons. One of the saloons, Dave Delyae's place, even had a cigar factory on its second floor.

Thompsonville got its own electrical power company in 1895, and civic boosters billed it as "the best lighted city in the United States." Social activities were extensive and varied. For those with refined tastes, there was an Opera House, and traveling stock companies put on such shows as Uncle Tom's Cabin. For sports enthusiasts there were professional prize fights and baseball games.

By 1910 most of the timber was gone, and Thompsonville went into decline. The Opera House, which became the Maccabee Hall, sat in disuse for decades, and was finally torn down in 1972. By the 1950s, the trains had stopped running. The population had dwindled to around two hundred by the early 1970s. The town, which was once an electric light hot spot for the nation is now far out of the limelight, serving primarily as a quiet place to retire and as a bedroom community to Traverse City. There has been a slight rebound in population. At nearby Crystal Mountain, where loggers once held the terrain in low regard, Crystal Mountain Resort, the largest private employer in Benzie County, has blossomed into one of the premier resorts in northern Michigan.

Honor

The father of Honor Gifford, shown here at the age of fifteen in 1909, named the town after her. Courtesy Congregational Summer Assembly.

An English industrialist, Joseph A. Gifford, thought so much of the opportunity he saw in the Platte River Valley that he named the town he founded there in 1895 for his dear daughter. Honor was her name, and for the next twenty years the town did her name proud.

Her father's Guelph Patent Cask Co., which made wooden containers from the plentiful maple in the area, attracted the Manistee and Northeastern and the Pere Marquette railroads, which in those days were always hungry for new business. The M&NE also provided passenger service. Log piles several times higher than a man's head lined both sides of the Platte River. Lumberjacks who had run out of trees to cut down in areas near the shores of Lake Michigan flocked to town. Within a couple of years, the population was nearly 1,000.

In 1908, the economic and political influence of Honor on the county was so great that the county seat was moved there. A cement block building for the sheriff's residence and office was built. The business of the courts was held on the second floor of a downtown store. But in 1916, with the timber nearly gone, leaving scarred and barren hillsides up and down the valley, the town lost its influence and the courthouse was moved to Beulah on Crystal Lake, which by then was the new up and coming town in the county. Today, the sheriff's building in Honor is a private residence that goes largely unnoticed, except for the seeming incongruity of bars on some of the windows.

Honor has been fortunate in that it is located on U.S. 31. The traffic on the highway has provided an economic lifeline. New businesses are generally tourist related. The river and nearby lakes attract thousands of fishermen each year. The Platte River Anadromous State Fish Hatchery, the state's largest, was built there in 1974, after it had been demonstrated that Pacific

The Guelph Patent Cask Co. on the Platte River at Honor used up almost all the area's hardwood and then closed shop. Courtesy Benzie Area Historical Museum.

The first settler in Lake Ann, A. P. Wheelock, named the town after his wife. Courtesy Vera Carmien.

salmon could thrive in the Great Lakes. The state Department of Natural Resources annually releases 5.5 million Chinook salmon and 1.8 million Coho salmon raised at the Honor facility into Michigan streams.

Lake Ann

Lake Ann was rebuilt after it was all but destroyed by fire in 1897, the day before what was to be a spanking Fourth of July celebration. The town was in decline but still game after a second fire in 1914, but when it burned a third time, in 1918, all but a handful of residents decided that living in the smallest incorporated village in Michigan had lost its appeal.

There were still only a handful of people living there in the 1960s when Sue Frost, who is a part of a renewal of the town's economy with her Firm Footings Children's Center, was growing up. "The roads were mostly gravel," she said. "Kids could play anywhere they wanted. Nobody worried about cars. There were houses with nobody living in them."

In the last twenty-five years or so, people from urban areas who have moved north to escape the rat race have discovered it. It is a half-hour drive from Traverse City, northwest Michigan's dominant city. The population of the town itself, still the smallest incorporated village in Michigan, is only about two hundred and fifty, but if the people in the whole of Almira Township who count themselves as Lake Ann residents were included, it would be several times larger. The town has even become a bit chic; a restaurant on First Street is called the L. A. Café, a play on Los Angeles. And the history of L. A., Michigan, has become a community preoccupation. A claim frequently heard, without much evidence to support it, is that during the lumbering boom Lake Ann challenged Traverse City as the most important town in the Grand Traverse region.

From its beginning shortly before the Civil War, Lake Ann has more closely identified with nearby Traverse City than with larger Benzie County

The Big Wheel, manufactured in Manistee, was a major advance in logging technology. A stack of logs was chained to the axle and when the tongue was lowered it acted as a lever, lifting one end of the stack so it could be dragged. Courtesy the Joy Family.

Fortunes were made during the lumber boom and many fine homes were built. When the boom went bust, some of the owners could no longer afford to maintain them. This house in Frankfort was torn down in 1949 and the boards were used to build a store. Courtesy Robert L. McCall.

towns. Before Almira Township was organized in 1894, there were a number of settlers, mostly subsistence farmers, living in the area who depended on Traverse City for their supplies. The first Lake Ann settler was A. P. Wheelock. He built a cabin beside the lake and gave it his wife's name. Almira Township was named after the wife of another early settler, A. J. Burrell.

As with other towns away from the shore of Lake Michigan, Lake Ann needed a railroad to prosper, and it got it with the Manistee & Northeastern. The present township hall is built on the location of the old depot. There had been a gristmill on a creek, named after Elijah Ransom who built it, and several small logging operations. The railroad made it profitable for William Habbeler, who came from Ohio, to build a large sawmill. It was the town's principal industry. The mill and scores of other buildings burned in the first fire. The general store and the blacksmith's shop are the only mill buildings remaining. The blacksmith's shop is to become a part of a new community museum. The store is now the Lake Ann Grocery, run by village newcomers John and Sandy Nuske, who serve cappuccino to morning commuters to Traverse City.

Lifelong resident James Morse recalls what it was like in 1934 when the railroad stopped running because all the quality timber had been cut. "When my father built a barn that year, the lumber was shipped in from Kingsport, Tennessee," he said. People nowadays have learned from the devastation of early-day logging, he said . . . Right now I've got my grandsons helping me plant blue spruce where Habbeler cut down the first growth."

Honor

Veterans of the Civil War, many of whom settled in Benzie County, were active until well into the twentieth century. A group of them in Honor, with the village band in the back row, posed for a photograph around 1890. Norman Covey Collection.

Big men were in large supply in the lumbering towns. Some of the biggest in Honor, boasting an average weight of 236 pounds, got together for a group portrait. Norman Covey Collection.

A Civil War veterans' parade was a summer highlight. Norman Covey Collection.

Dr. Israel P. Covey, who had been a Civil War medical officer, established a practice in Honor in 1895. Norman Covey Collection.

The proverbial horse and buggy of the family doctor was used to make house calls. Norman Covey Collection.

By the 1920s, horses were being phased out. The hitching rails were gone, replaced by angle parking for Model T Fords in Honor. Norman Covey Collection.

As a young man (previous page), Honor pharmacist Ezra Covey had a fine rig. Later (left), he owned the first car in Honor. Norman Covey Collection.

When it was established in 1895, Honor was a single-industry town with the Guelph Patent Cask Co. Stacks of logs line the Platte River for use in the mill. Norman Covey Collection.

A shift crew at Guelph takes a break to have its picture taken. Norman Covey Collection.

The jumble of houses of a lumbering town like Honor indicates the haste at which they were built to accommodate workers. Courtesy Benzie Area Historical Museum.

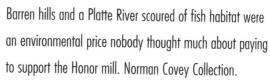

Barren hills and a Platte River scoured of fish habitat were
an environmental price nobody thought much about paying
to support the Honor mill. Norman Covey Collection.

Elberta

The schooner Isolda Buck picks up a load of lumber at the Crane Lumber Co. near Elberta. Allen Blacklock Collection.

A logging crew poses outside
an Elberta boarding house after
they had driven logs down
the Betsie River to Betsie Bay.
Allen Blacklock Collection.

The Eagle Hotel in Elberta was
built around the turn of the
century. Later it became a lodge
hall and members of the lodge
crowded together for a picture.
Allen Blacklock Collection.

Glarum's General Store was
an Elberta landmark in the
1920s as the lumbering boom
was coming to an end. Courtesy
Mrs. John W. Peterson.

The Fourth of July was a raucous time in towns like Elberta, a time as this 1912 celebration shows, for local swains to kick up a little dust and fly the flag. Allen Blacklock Collection.

No self-respecting town felt it was complete without a marching band.
Elberta was no exception. Allen Blacklock Collection.

Wooden butter bowls, which were used before
the advent of paper containers, were manufactured
at Knapp's Woodenware factory on Betsie
Bay. Courtesy Benzie Area Historical Museum.

Lake Ann

There's a bit of irony in the display of a sign in the Lake Ann general store window ("God Bless Our Firemen") in a 1975 picture. The town burned three times during the lumbering era. Courtesy Vera Carmien.

Lake Ann was not without is refinements. It even had a string quartet. Courtesy Vera Carmien.

A passenger train chugs into Lake Ann on the Manistee & Northeastern Railroad around 1900. Courtesy Vera Carmien.

There were no paved roads into Lake Ann at the turn of the century, but the way through town was wide.
Courtesy Vera Carmien.

A horse-drawn U.S. Post Office wagon waits at the new Lake Ann depot for the arrival of the town's mail from Traverse City. Courtesy Vera Carmien.

One of the earliest settlers in the Lake Ann area was Elijah Ransom, shown in 1890 with his wife, Edna, and, in descending order, their children: Francis, John Emma, Ebenezer, and Leland. Courtesy Vera Carmien.

After the last of three fires, Lake Ann almost became a ghost town. One of the places to burn was the Douglas Hotel. Courtesy Vera Carmien.

Habbeler's Mill, which put Lake Ann on the map, burned in 1897, starting the town on a downward spiral. Courtesy Vera Carmien.

Lumbermen took pride in the number of logs they could stack on a sled and worried later about whether the team could pull the weight. Courtesy Vera Carmien.

The Rev. John H. Grant, one of the ministers who was active in the early years of the Congregational Summer Assembly on Crystal Lake and Lake Michigan, was not afraid to go out on a limb, as he did here on a high sandbluff. Courtesy Congregational Summer Assembly.

CHAPTER 4 CRYSTAL LAKE AND BEULAH

*"The attractiveness of Crystal Lake has been increasingly appreciated
as it has become known . . . It is recognized as not only the most
beautiful of the many small lakes in which Michigan abounds, but also
as unsurpassed, if indeed equaled, in the whole country."*

**From Attractions of Crystal Lake and Vicinity by the
Rev. Frank T. Lee of the Congregational Summer Assembly, 1923.**

It's a mid-May day, and Crystal Lake is at its pristine best. Sparkles of late afternoon sun tapdance on calm waters. Whispers of summer waft on honeyed spring breezes. Adding a comely accent to the reverie of the set piece is a young woman pushing her two toddlers on the swing set on the public beach.

The woman calls to her husband, who is concentrating on pacing off the distance—a matter of some one hundred and fifty feet—from the water's edge to an historic marker by a picnic table in the park on the other side of the shore-line road.

"What are you doing?" she asks. "We drove all the way from Grand Rapids to get here. Come take the kids' picture. This is a day to remember."

"Be there in a minute," he says, snapping a picture of the historical marker. "Can you imagine what it must have been like before?"

"Before what?" She joins him at the marker with kids in tow.

"Before this happened." He points to the marker. It reads:

*In 1873 an ambitious but ill-advised project was put through in an
effort to connect Crystal Lake and Lake Michigan with a navigable channel.
The original level of Crystal Lake was, at that time, much higher than its*

present level. The project was a complete failure in respect to its accomplishing it proposed purpose. The result was the lowering of the lake and exposing a wide stretch of beach around the entire lake and making possible the development of Crystal Lake as a resort and residential area as well as the site of the village of Beulah. This monument erected by the people of Benzie County, stands at the original level of Crystal Lake.

In an era ruled by environmental impact statement and engineering exactitude, the cavalier unplugging of a sand barrier so Crystal Lake could join the flow of the Betsie River to Lake Michigan one Saturday morning in September 1873, is difficult to imagine. Also difficult to comprehend is that even though a 1922 historical account by Leonard L. Case was entitled The *Tragedy of Crystal Lake,* it turned out for the best, both economically and aesthetically. The perpetrator of the ill-advised project was a Merengo, Illinois, farmer and businessman named Archibald Jones who came north during the lumber boom to seek his fortune.

Jones wanted to provide a way to transport hemlock bark by boat for the tanning industry and hardwood to satisfy the insatiable appetite for wood to make charcoal for the Frankfort Iron Works (1870–1883) ore smelting operation on the south shore of Betsie Bay.

When the Betsie River Improvement Co., with a coterie of willing investors, was formed in the summer of 1873, Crystal Lake resembled a Scottish loch, a bit forbidding, with steep, tree-covered shores. There were marshes but virtually no beaches. The digging of the channel began almost immediately after the company was formed. Initially, plans also called for opening a channel linking Crystal Lake to Platte Lake to the north. Curiously, Jones seemingly had little doubt about the practicality of the channel from Crystal Lake to the Betsie—it's doubtful that even a rudimentary engineering study was done—but when it came to linking with the Platte surveyors were called in. They found that the channel would actually drain Crystal Lake into Platte Lake, rather than vice versa, and that phase of the project was abandoned.

Beulah, shown here in 1892, was made possible by a man-made flood in 1873 that permanently lowered the level of Crystal Lake, exposing miles of new beach-front. Courtesy Benzie Area Historical Museum.

The channel from Crystal Lake to the Betsie was opened on a Saturday afternoon in September 1873. It went from a trickle to a torrent within an hour, smashing out of the river channel and flooding the surrounding countryside. The roar was heard five miles away in Benzonia. Roads were washed out and travel between Benzonia and Frankfort came to a halt. Logs in the river that were being floated to Frankfort were strewn over several square miles. A horse and buggy driven by a Baptist minister, the Rev. Adoniram

Joy (after whom Joyfield Township is named), was caught in the flood and the minister nearly drowned. Within days, Crystal Lake was diminished by 2,000 acres to its present 9,711 acres. It is eight miles long and two and three miles wide.

The once dour lake, which has always been a primary focal point for Benzie County (Crystal Lake Township originally encompassed the entire county), was transformed into what ultimately became a more pleasing and pastoral presence.

As the lake was lowered by about ten feet, the channel quickly filled with sand and the Betsie again became unnavigable for large boats. Hundreds of acres of new shoreline were exposed. Beaches appeared where none had been before. The Rev. Charles E. Bailey, the founder of Benzonia and always one to recognize the next best opportunity, bought large tracts of the new beachfront. In 1890 he would found Beulah, a Biblical name chosen because it denoted future prosperity when the Israelites applied it to Jerusalem. (The original official name of the settlement—Crystal City and the Beulah Vista Resort—was unwieldy and was soon shortened to just plain Beulah, which is what everybody had been calling it anyway.)

All this and more had Archibald Jones unknowingly wrought. Although he returned to Merengo thinking of himself as a failure, in his wake he left the makings for developments that would change the very character of Benzie County. Beulah would someday (in 1916) become the county seat.

The beaches attracted tourists. Cottages were built around the lake. A pre-World War II brochure advertising vacation cottages available at Robinson's Cold Brook Inn gives an idea of the sorts of lodgings that were available. There were the Little Tin Cottage, with "water at the back door," for $15 a week; Babcock Cottage, with two stories and a large porch, for $27.50 a week, and the Crystal Perch, with one bed and a path through the woods to the beach, for $10 a week. For the more affluent, there was Hill Crest, with a fireplace, a large porch overlooking the lake and—to top it off—a "dining room with good dishes."

An open boat from Terp's Pavilion would go around Crystal Lake picking up people for an evening dance and then take them back to their cottages. Courtesy Benzie Area Historical Museum.

Congregationalists from throughout the Midwest would form the Congregational Summer Assembly, one of the most successful religious endeavors of its type in the country. Crystal Downs, a world-renowned golf course, whose charm relies on vistas overlooking both Crystal Lake and Lake Michigan, would follow. And not least of all, families like the one from Grand Rapids, would hear of Crystal Lake's reputation as one of the most beautiful lakes in Creation.

Beulah

In the summer after the man-made flood, Western Union extended a telegraph line from Traverse City to Frankfort, using the new shoreline as part of the right of way. As commercial and residential development followed, Benzonians watched uneasily from their hilltop redoubt. Beulah from the beginning was a challenge to the Puritan principles of the area's early Congregational settlers; Benzonia catered to worshippers, Beulah to funsters. (Beulah and Benzonia operated as a single municipality, a fractious arrangement that existed until 1932 when Beulah broke away and incorporated separately.)

Not surprisingly, the first person to build a house in Beulah was Rev. Bailey, who had returned to the area after having moved away for several years because of differences with other original colonists. The house with an imposing number of gables is still a residence on Crystal Avenue. In 1889 the Frankfort and Southeast Railroad (later the Ann Arbor) was built along the south shore, a routing which would have been impossible without the debacle of 1873. Beulah thus became a tourist destination, much to the benefit of Bailey and his family, who served lemonade to the railroad work crews.

Beulah was soon outstripping Benzonia in growth. In 1892 even though Beulah and Benzonia were corporately one, Beulah got its own post office. It was probably the only municipality in the United States to have two post offices. At the turn of the century, a commercial district was taking shape on Benzie Boulevard. The Beulah Drug Co. and Central State Bank (both still in business), a grocery store, livery stables, and other businesses served the growing population and vacationers.

Among the first of several resort hotels was the Windemere, built on the waterfront a mile north of the town in 1903. It was sold in 1911 to ten Jewish families and served as a private club until the 1950s when it was torn down to make room for two private residences. The fifty-room Northway was opened in 1920 and was operated for many years by Frank Orcutt, a primary booster of Beulah in its early glory days.

Tourism was so successful in Beulah that the Ann Arbor Railroad extended a line to the community. Courtesy Benzie Area Historical Museum.

Probably best remembered by old-timers is Terp's Pavilion, which from the early 1920s through World War II, was the Beulah hot spot. Archibald Ethelbert Terpening provided activities the proper Benzonians frowned upon. There was a live band for dancing. It had bowling, roller-skating, machines to test a young man's punch, slot machines, and picture shows. Terpening ran an excursion boat from the beach of his Crystal Lake emporium to the resorts and cottages around the lake to pick up customers.

Robert Kirshner Jr., whose family has vacationed on Crystal Lake since 1902, recalls stories from those early days.

"The Pathfinder boat from Terp's would go around the lake and pick up people and take them to the dance," he said. "Those were great times."

An earlier amusement center venture didn't fare so well. It was called "The Grand" and was designed by the same architect who built the Grand Hotel on Mackinac Island. The large building dominated the downtown, as it still does to this day, although presently it is privately owned and not open to the public. As part of its effort to get the county seat moved to Beulah, the town bought it for a courthouse. Extensive remodeling was done to accommodate its new function, including adding a new facade with a clock over the entrance by which residents still get the time of day. It served as the county's courthouse until 1976, when it was replaced by a new government complex on U.S. 31, east of town.

Development was not restricted to Beulah proper. Rental cottages and what today would be called bed-and-breakfast inns dotted the shoreline. Many of them later reverted to cottages, as the lake gained in popularity. Many of the lakeside cottages have been converted to year-round retirement homes. There are two summer camps with religious affiliations still in operation. They are the Congregational Summer Assembly (see below) and the 160-acre Crystal Conference Center founded in 1918 and owned by the Christian Church (Disciples of Christ) Michigan Region. Crystal Conference Center is now a non-denominational camp for children and a limited number of families. In the off seasons, it is used for religious retreats. It no longer is a cottage community, having sold off that part of its holdings.

There once were several non-religious summer camps. Only one remains. It is Crystalaire Camp, founded as Camp Osoha of the Dunes in the early 1920s as a girls' camp by Mrs. B. G. Mattson, the wife of a

Charlevoix minister. Morristow Hills, which made summer memorable for children for more than twenty years, closed in 1953.

Congregational Summer Assembly

During the first years of the Congregational Summer Assembly, some members camped in tents during their summer sojourns. The woman at the far left is Mrs. Charles H. Kirshner, whose family is still active in the assembly. Courtesy Congregational Summer Assembly.

For several decades before the turn of the century, vacationers had been coming to Frankfort by lake steamers, mainly from Chicago and Milwaukee, but towns in the interior had not benefited because of relative inaccessibility.

In 1900 the railroad, which had previously (in 1892) instituted a cross-lake ferry service out of Frankfort and was preparing to build the Royale Frontenac Hotel there, extended service to Beulah with the intention of changing the pattern. Given the influence of the Congregational Church, it was perhaps foreordained that the railroad would strike a bargain with the church.

As it happened, the Cleveland Conference of Congregational Churches of Ohio was considering establishing a summer meeting place, a common practice among Protestant denominations of the time. The Congregational churches had been meeting at Lakeside, Ohio, on Lake Erie, where the dominant influence was Methodist. They wanted a place of their own. At a meeting at Lakeside in the summer of 1902, the Congregational Summer Assembly was formed. Its goal was to find a place to "meet together in the summer for mutual acquaintance and fellowship, but more especially for a deeper and clearer understanding of the life and character of Jesus Christ and consequent increase of spiritual power." And, they might have added, a place away from city business where the kids could swim, the nights were cool for sleeping, and property values a bargain. In 1903, the Congregationalists held a summer meeting in tents on Lake Michigan near New Buffalo in southwest Michigan.

The meeting was moved in 1904 to Frankfort. Railroad officials, anxious to attract vacationers from points east along their rails, agreed in 1905 to give the assembly 163 acres, with frontage on both Crystal Lake and Lake Michigan. The only conditions were that for five years the assembly would attract at least 200 people a year (a number that more than doubled after two years) and that buildings with a combined worth of at least $10,000 would be constructed.

Over the years, the assembly has maintained its religious focus. It is still the sort of place that an early visitor like the Rev. Charles M. Sheldon, who wrote *In His Steps* (1896), a commentary on Jesus that at one time sold only slightly less well than the Bible, would probably still feel comfortable.

Vacationers would be picked up by horse-drawn bus in 1916 at the train depot and taken to the assembly grounds. Courtesy Congregational Summer Assembly.

The assembly grounds, which have since grown to about 200 acres, have been the permanent home of the assembly since 1906. There are about 145 cottages, athletic fields, a meeting hall and a chapel. Activities from June to September range from swimming, boating, tennis and softball to Bible studies, crafts, theatrical productions and concentrated loafing. More than 2,500 adults and children visited in the summer of 1996.

James Buzzell, a retired Frankfort teacher and athletic coach who has been the managing director for more than two decades, said the assembly provides continuity from generation to generation.

"What I like to hear from the people who come is that the place hasn't changed a bit," he said.

Crystal Downs

(Below) When Crystal Downs was built in 1927, a dirt road wound through what was to become one of the top golf courses in the world. Courtesy Robert L. McCall. (Bottom) Crystal Downs today is the golf course in northern Michigan top golfers want to play. Photo by Thomas BeVier.

Nearly a half-century after Walkley Ewing of Grand Rapids chanced upon the property that would become Crystal Downs Country Club, he clearly remembered the moment when he first saw it.

After hiking through snowdrifts in the winter of 1926, he recalled in a history of the club, he emerged through the woods and stood atop a dune, which provides views over the present eighteenth hole of Lake Michigan and Crystal Lake.

"That instant was really the birth of Crystal Downs," he said. " I had never in my life been so overwhelmed with the beauty of a land-and-seascape. I immediately felt that here was something too good merely to option for passing on to others who, more than likely, would desecrate it. Here was something worth developing and throwing one's self into in a full-time way. I proceeded to do so."

The 400-acre site, which includes the golf course and homes, took shape gradually. The Crystal Downs Country Club was incorporated in June 1927, the year after the first nine-hole course was built. Ewing and others were not particularly enchanted by those holes. By chance, in 1928, the foremost golf architect of the time, Dr. Alister MacKenzie of England, happened to be in America. Club leaders asked him to visit their site. He did so grudgingly. However, on the trip along the Lake Michigan shore from Grand Rapids to Frankfort, he was enchanted with the terrain, saying it reminded him of the Scottish and English seaside links country. He designed the present eighteen-hole course, which was completed in 1933.

In the early years, the club struggled financially, especially during World War II when gas rationing made travel difficult. A membership in the 1950s could be had for $300. Today the fee is many times more than that, and there is a long waiting list.

For decades Crystal Downs Country Club, a golfer's Scottish dream (or nightmare at times) with its rolling terrain, narrow fairways and unsympathetic rough, was one of the golfing fraternity's best kept secrets. That changed in the late 1970s, so the story goes, after professional golfer Ben Crenshaw, who finished second in the British Open in 1978 and 1979, was invited to play the course after he'd finished a tournament in the Detroit area. He spread the news and golf magazines were soon writing about the course. One proclaimed it as one of the ten most challenging in the world.

Members had mixed feelings about the publicity. After all, one of the club's charms was its privacy. It provided a place where the wealthy, near wealthy, and not so wealthy could meet in civil competition. Even though superlatives fail to describe the setting—rolling, tree-covered dunes set amid a watery vista—the homes set back from the winding and climbing roads through the complex make a pleasing argument against ostentatious display. Cocktails are served after five, and there is an almost old world emphasis on good behavior.

As is noted in the club's history, it's still a place to pause, perhaps on a "rapturous evening . . . with the moonlight shining a silver path across Crystal and listening to the murmur of the Big Lake behind you and sense that the Islands and Sleeping Bear are out there too." And to think, perhaps, "that this must not cease to be."

The first prayer meeting of the Congregational Summer Assembly in 1901 was held in a tent. Courtesy Charles Webb Fairchild Family.

Horseplay on the beach was as much a part of the summer on Crystal
Lake in the 1920s as it is today. There were rowboats to rent, and
there were sailboat races nearly every evening.
Courtesy Robert Kirshner.

The Ottawa Resort, shown in 1911, and the Crystal Beach Resort, shown in 1948, are two of scores that have come and gone on Crystal Lake. Many of the old cabins have been converted to permanent homes. Courtesy Robert Kirshner.

The Morristow Hills Camp, one of several children's camps on Crystal Lakes prior to World War II, stressed physical exercise. Courtesy Marion Stow.

A present-day Benzie County institution, the Cherry Hut restaurant in Beulah, started out in this little building on a gravel road. Courtesy Benzie Area Historical Museum.

Fifty years ago, the roads in Benzie County left a lot to be desired. A heavy rain could raise havoc, as it did in September 1941 with Larsen Lane. Courtesy Congregational Summer Assembly.

The most practical means of travel in the early days was by
train. Hotels were often built near a railroad. Here a train
steams past the Van Winkle Hotel in Beulah in the late 1890s.
Courtesy Benzie Area Historical Museum.

The fifty-room Northway Hotel at Beulah was one of several hotels
built in the early 1920s. It operated for fifty years. Courtesy Benzie
Area Historical Society.

In the 1940s, a miniature train that ran on a small oval track near Beulah was popular with families on Crystal Lake. Courtesy Congregational Summer Assembly.

Between 1900 and 1975, downtown
Beulah underwent tremendous change,
but the pace has never gotten out of hand.
Courtesy Benzie Area Historical Museum.

The snapshot of children going to the beach on Crystal Lake could as easily been taken today as it was in the 1920s. Courtesy Robert Kirshner.

CHAPTER 5 FRANKFORT AND THE RAILROAD CAR FERRIES

Gateway to the former Ann Arbor Car Ferry Fleet.
A Growing City. Always in Season.

Message on the arch over the highway just east of Frankfort

As nearly a century of cross-lake railroad car ferry service came to an end in Frankfort, the Michigan Department of Transportation decided that the town should also, in effect, forfeit its bragging rights by removing the arch over the highway on the hill that dips down to the village proper.

The two pillars on both sides of the road, fashioned to resemble lighthouses, had to come down to allow for widening Michigan 115, the state said. That meant that the span with a model of the *City of Green Bay* car ferry on top also would go and with it—at least symbolically—a mainstay of Frankfort's heritage. That was in 1983. It was coincidental that the widening of the highway and the demise of the car ferries coincided. Still, it was as if the state was adding insult to injury.

It had been only a few months since April 1982 when the last car ferry left Frankfort, leaving a huge void in the area's economic base. The loss also did immeasurable damage to the community's identity. As nearly every school child could tell, in 1892 the world's first ferry service over a large expanse of open water—the sixty-three miles from Frankfort to Keewaunee, Wisconsin—began in Frankfort. If pressed, a student might even have been able to provide the exact date, November 24, 1892.

(Car ferry service was subsequently instituted at other West Michigan towns, including Ludington, Grand Haven, and Muskegon. Only the Ludington service to Manitowoc, Wisconsin, which began in 1897, is now operating with a single boat, the S.S. *Badger.* Unlike the original service, it depends on automobiles and passengers, rather than railroad cars.)

The *Ann Arbor Number Two* railroad car ferry in the foreground was one of two put into service to cross Lake Michigan in 1892 at South Frankfort (later Elberta) on Betsie Bay. It was the first time a ferry service had covered a large, open expanse of water. The wooded hill in the center of the picture is where the Royale Frontenac Hotel was built in 1900. Courtesy Benzie Shores District Library.

Even though tourism, lumbering and its related industries and agriculture were important factors in Frankfort's economy early in the twentieth century, it was the car ferries that gave it heft. The influence of the boats, which were among the most prominent on the Great Lakes, was more than just economic. There was—and continues to be—an emotional attachment. One Frankfort native recalled that as the last of the car ferries were phased out, people would gather on the beach and watch them go. "They'd have tears in their eyes," he said.

Topped with a model of a railroad car ferry on the span, the Gateway Arch was built in 1925 on the east end of downtown Frankfort. It was moved in 1937 to the top of the hill approaching the town on Michigan 115. Courtesy Robert Kirshner.

And so the community fought the state's proposal to remove the Gateway Arch. Letters were sent to politicians and bureaucrats, editorials were written and opposition was voiced at public meetings. Frankfort had had a Gateway Arch since 1925 (first in downtown Frankfort and later, beginning in 1937, over the highway). People weren't about to let the state tear it down. The arch remains to this day.

What is sometimes overlooked, is that with the advent of the car ferries another grand Great Lakes tradition—the sailing ship—was displaced as a primary presence in the harbor. The sailing schooners reigned through the first part of the lumber boom, from the 1860s to past the turn of the century. When the timber ran out, so did their usefulness and so did the role of men like Dan Seavy, captain of the Wanderer, one of the last of the schooners. Stories persist of his toughness—he battered a man insensible on the ice of Betsie Bay in 1904—and of other oddities, not the least of which being the practice of piracy.

The car ferries did something for the area the sailing schooners had not, according to Florence Bixby, a former Frankfort teacher and a past curator of the Benzie Area Historical Society.

"The Ann Arbor with its ferries did more than just carry freight and passengers," she said. "The railroad advertised the beauty of the county—its lakes and fishing—all over the country. It put Benzie County on the map."

As an aside, she said it also aggravated the dissension between Frankfort and Elberta. On the Elberta side were the car ferry docks, grain elevators, warehouses, and other industrial facilities. People who lived there were mainly working class. On the Frankfort side there were hotels for tourists, a more viable shopping district, and more comely neighborhoods.

"You could tell the difference at elections," Mrs. Bixby said, with a chuckle. "People in Elberta tended to vote for Democrats, and Frankfort was a Republican stronghold."

Railroads dominated commerce throughout the nation until after World War II, and Betsie Bay shared the spotlight. Passengers flocked to the two depots the Ann Arbor had on Betsie Bay by 1899. One was in Frankfort and the other in South Frankfort (South Frankfort became Elberta in 1911). Trains on the spur line into Frankfort would drop off tourists and other passengers and then back around the bay and go into Elberta, where the car ferries waited to take freight cars, passengers, and automobiles across the lake. The car ferries cut a day or two off the time it took to get to Wisconsin because they made it unnecessary to go down to Chicago and back up on the western shore of Lake Michigan.

The ferry system was the idea of James M. Ashley, an Ohio politician who had served briefly as governor of the Montana Territory. He began construction of the first two car ferries and terminals in South Frankfort and Keewaunee two years before the ferries went into service and even before his Ann Arbor Railroad had acquired the Frankfort and Southeastern Railroad that ran from the lumbering town of Thompsonville to Betsie Bay. The investment was an extraordinary display of confidence in an idea that many people said was impractical, especially during the winter because of Lake Michigan's ice.

The first car ferry was the *Ann Arbor Number One.* It cost $260,000 to build, a princely sum in those days. It was made of oak with steel sheathing and was 267 feet long with a fifty-two-foot beam. A magazine article printed an artist's drawing of the new boat, with the following description: "The engraving represents a novel vessel, the first of its kind, recently built for a railway company to transfer freight cars from Michigan to Wisconsin without breaking bulk. This is done by carrying the cars bodily over a distance of 63 miles across a dark and stormy water and through ice which is of thickness and solidity from 18 inches upward . . . They carry 24 loaded freight cars at each trip a very respectable train, and they make the run—63 miles in four hours, 30 minutes—say 14 miles an hour . . ."

On its first trip, with four railroad carloads of coal, *Number One* ran aground on the Wisconsin side. It took two days to free the boat, and it returned with twenty-two cars of flour. Despite the difficulty, the inauguration was hailed as a success and soon other Lake Michigan ports were added in Wisconsin and in the Upper Peninsula. *Number One* survived several more groundings and being stuck in the ice before it burned and sank in Manitowoc, Wisconsin, on March 8, 1910. The *Ann Arbor Number Two* was in service until 1916 when it was declared obsolete. It was rebuilt for dredging.

The *Ann Arbor Number Three* was the first all-steel car ferry. Besides being able to haul railroad cars, it also had a hold for grain. It could accommodate 300 travelers. In the 1930s, it was cut down and used as a scow and barge before finally being scrapped.

By 1928, there were six car ferries sailing out of Betsie Bay. They made 4,300 cross-lake trips with 10,000 freight cars. As the service had become more established, the boats seemed to take on personality. Some even got distinctive names. One was the *Wabash,* which was commissioned in 1927. It was 380 feet long, with a beam of 57 1/2 feet and had amenities lacking on other boats. There were staterooms for forty passengers, some with private parlors and bathrooms; a ladies' room, a smoking room, and a dining room. It could carry 380 deck passengers. Quarters for the crew were improved. Later, it was renamed the *City of Green Bay.* It was decommissioned in 1974 and sold for scrap.

The Great Lakes often made for uneasy sailing. The boats frequently went aground. There were collisions with other boats, fierce storms and—in the winter—the constant peril of ice. An occasional untoward incident was to be expected. The *Ann Arbor Number Four,* however, had more than its share of problems. It went into service in 1906 and soon became known as a hard-luck boat. Allen Blacklock, in his history of Elberta, provided a long list of its mishaps. Among the more spectacular accidents listed were rolling onto its side in Manistique while loading iron ore railroad cars, going onto the beach in both Manitowoc and Green Bay and sinking twice. It sank the first time at Manitowoc and the second time at Elberta. It was raised and put back in service both times. In 1937, bruised and bent, *Number Four* was sold to the state of Michigan and renamed the *Cheboygan.* It served out its days as a car ferry at the Straits of Mackinac until the bridge over the straits was opened in 1957.

With black smoke huffing from its stacks, three car ferries struggle to make a way through the Lake Michigan ice in 1902. Courtesy Lois Bender.

The *Ann Arbor Number Five* was known as the "Bull of the Woods" for its ability to break ice. It served from 1910 to about 1960 before being scrapped. *Number Six* joined the fleet in 1917 and was renamed the *Arthur K. Atkinson,* after a railroad executive. It was the largest (after a thirty-four-foot lengthening) at 384 feet and it was the first boat on the Great Lakes with a 5,000-horsepower engine. Because of mechanical problems, it was docked in the 1970s. The problems were deemed too expensive to repair and it was scrapped.

Number Seven, called the *Viking,* was the last boat, launched in 1925. It ended its life as a gambling ship in Canada.

Bill Bacon, who was in charge of the ferry service nearly until its demise, spent his life on the boats. During his boyhood, his father, an engineer on the ferries, often took him along on weekends and holidays. In 1948 Bacon himself shipped out as an ordinary seaman and he quickly moved up in rank. He became the port captain in 1963. The operation was in its heyday then, employing more than 350 workers at union wages, which were relatively high for Benzie County.

"The death of the car ferries was inevitable," he said. "I saw it coming in the 1960s when the railroads started going to hell. When we lost Ford freight (from Wisconsin plants) in 1960, that was the beginning of the end."

Railroad cars and automobiles vied for space on the car ferries. Here the last passengers before departure board the *Ann Arbor Number Five* for the trip across Lake Michigan to the Wisconsin shore. Courtesy Benzie Area Historical Museum.

A car ferry, framed in a gap in the Lake Michigan sand dunes near Frankfort known as the Devil's Arm Chair, starts its sixty-three-mile trek to Wisconsin. Courtesy Charles Webb Fairchild Family.

The *John D. Dewar* was a passenger and freight boat that sailed out of the Frankfort harbor to Empire and Manistee. In this 1904 photograph, Hattie Robertson, whose father, Henry F. Robertson owned the boat, sits on a bench in front of the pilot house with an unidentified man. Courtesy Frances P. Larson.

There were a number of factors involved. The old ferries were designed to carry forty-foot boxcars, but by the 1950s the industry standard was ninety feet. The rail yards in Chicago were made more efficient in moving railroad cars so cross-lake shipping lost much of its economic advantage. On October 2, 1977, the Ann Arbor transferred ownership to the Michigan Interstate Railway Co., a company cobbled together with support from state government.

Many people realized that an era was almost over. Some tried to be philosophical about it. Leonard Case, who had a column called *The Crystal Gazer* in the Benzie County *Ad-Visor*, considered a worst-case scenario and then offered the following:

"If, in the loss of a railroad, Benzie County would gain an attractive and properly maintained wilderness area, free from the devastating inroads of progress, the loss might prove to be a blessing in disguise."

His philosophizing didn't provide much comfort.

The car ferries sailed year-round. In the winter, ice often took its toll. Repairs are being made here to the *Ann Arbor Number Three*. Courtesy Charles Webb Fairchild family.

IMAGES OF BENZIE COUNTY

These three pictures, all taken around the turn of the century, show sailing schooners aground in Lake Michigan near Frankfort. Within a few years, such boats would pass into history, replaced by steam-powered vessels. Courtesy Benzie Area Historical Museum and Lillie Blacklock.

No local scrapbook is complete
without dramatic pictures
of ice covered boats. The boat
with the hole in its hull is
the *Ann Arbor Number Four,* which
sank at the Elberta pier in
1923. Courtesy Ena V. Jackson.

The absolute end came in 1982, when the *Atkinson,* with crowds looking quietly on, was towed out of the harbor. The damage to the economy had already been done over the previous years, as the boats were phased out. Benzie County, which at one time had had among the highest per capita incomes in northwest Michigan, by then had one of the lowest. Businesses struggled. Some failed.

There is still resentment. The railroads failed to modernize, people say. The state should have done more. The unions, with their insistence on high wages, made the operation unprofitable. There are few subjects of conversation in Frankfort that can so easily ignite old emotions.

"It didn't have to happen," said a middle-aged man during a discussion at a downtown Frankfort business.

"Hey, what was the exact date when the last car ferry left?" someone asked him.

"April 26, 1982," he said, without pause. "It's a day I'll never forget."

For nearly a century, from 1892 until 1982, the Ann Arbor Railroad's car ferries were pervasive on Betsie Bay. Local people learned to tell them apart by whether their stacks were slanted or straight. Number Five was known as a good icebreaker. Number Four was accident-prone. By the 1970s, it was apparent that their days were numbered. The boat being towed out of the harbor for the last time is the *Viking*, which ended its life as a gambling ship in Canada. Courtesy Benzie Area Historical Museum.

The Ann Arbor Railroad had several hundred employees.
One of the pictures shows the workers at the repair shop and
the other shows employees who went on strike in 1888.
Allen Blacklock Collection.

The Ann Arbor Railroad had two tall grain elevators in 1910. The large boat with the two smoking stacks is a passenger ship in front of the Royale Frontenac Hotel. Courtesy Benzie Shores District Library.

Shortly after the Frankfort Harbor was dredged and piers were built, the U.S. Life Saving Service established a station on the Elberta side of the harbor. An early crew posed in front of the first station with their firefighting equipment. (Courtesy Benzie Area Historical Museum.) The station was later modernized, but life saving boats still depended on the brawn of rowers. (Courtesy Benzie Shores District Library.) The duties of the Life Saving Service are now handled by the U.S. Coast Guard, which has a station on the Frankfort side of the harbor.

CHAPTER 6 PEACHES AND OTHER FRUITS

The soil (in Benzie County) is a warm, sandy and gravely loam, very productive, and suitable for all kinds of grains and vegetables . . . The soil is especially adapted to fruit culture . . .

From The Grand Traverse Region, published in 1884.

Percy Smeltzer's great-grandfather came to Benzie County in 1872.

"He had farmed in Ontario," said Smeltzer, whose own livelihood has depended on the county's fickle soil for all his seventy-seven years. "The timber companies had cut most of the timber. They said that it must be great land because the trees were so big. They couldn't have been more mistaken."

His great-grandfather was wooed, as were many others, by reports that "all crops are raised in profusion," be they wheat, corn, oats, rye, or barley; potatoes, turnips, carrots, or celery, to select from a long list cited in an early report on the county's agricultural vigor.

Smeltzer scoffs at those early claims. He knows from experience how fragile an occupation farming can be in the county. He has witnessed the decline of dairy and cash crop farming and the demise of peaches. He's seen scores of family farms fail, unable to compete as the marketplace went from being regional to national in scope.

The survival of his own family in agriculture has sometimes been touch-and-go.

"In the 1930s, we had a large dairy farm," he said. "We pasteurized our own milk and even made ice cream. I went to Michigan State and graduated in 1942 with a degree in dairy manufacturing. Six days after I graduated, I went into the Army. When I came back in the spring in 1946, the dairy industry was gone. We planted our fields in fruit, apples, and cherries."

Even though Benzie County is blessed with lakes and streams, it was often difficult to dig successful wells. Some pioneer farmers had to haul water by barrel. Owen Sherwood and his team of oxen are shown in 1907 delivering water to the Twiddle Farm on the Benzie-Leelanau County line. Courtesy Benzie Shores District Library.

After loggers had finished cutting the trees, farmers built rude cabins and attempted to make a living farming the sandy soils. Some succeeded; many did not. The Nugent family, shown in front of their Joyfield Township cabin in 1895, prospered against all odds, and their descendants are today prominent in Benzie County agriculture. From left are Mary and Wesley Nugent and their children: Leo, Herb and Howard. In 1914 the family moved to a new farmhouse in Blaine Township. By 1917, when this photograph was taken, they had had six more children: Charlie, Hazel, Lloyd, Bill, Sylvia and Guy. Later they had four more (Chester, Davis, Louis and Zella) bringing the total to thirteen. Courtesy Mary and Wesley Nugent Family.

Today his family—his brother, Clinton, and their sons also are involved—annually grow a million pounds of tart cherries, 150,000 bushels of apples, and a small amount of sweet cherries. The family-owned Smeltzer Orchard Co., with 200 employees during the peak season, freezes and dries sixteen million pounds of cherries annually. It is one of two fruit processing operations in the county. (Graceland Fruit has the largest fruit drying capacity in the United States. Another pioneer family, the Nugents, owns it.)

Smeltzer's forebears and other settlers discovered that the bare soils left in the wake of the timber barons were over-rated. A typical story was told by an Inland Township pioneer as he described the fate of a neighbor: "George entered a 40-acre homestead . . . but soon abandoned it and returned to Ohio with the story that grass would not grow in this country even in the door yards." And in Benzonia Township, a supervisor reported in 1897 that "the first few crops of wheat were so filled with smut as to be almost useless for flour and worthless as a crop," although he did boast that one farmer had grown a twenty-four pound beet.

"Those early descriptions of the land sound like they were written by a real estate agent," said L. Andrew Norman, who for more than twenty years has been the agent in Benzie County for the Michigan State University Cooperative Extension Service. "It (claims of fertility) may have been true for a season or two, but the soil was quickly depleted . . . There are some pockets of good ground here and there, but they are few and far between." He points out that during the Depression huge tracts of land in the central part of the county was deemed so unsuited to agriculture that owners allowed their land to revert to the state rather than pay property taxes. One claim that has stood the test of time, he said, is the suitability for orchards, but even there the county's statewide status for fruit growing has diminished. It ranks forty-first among the state's eighty-three counties in fruit production.

A threshing crew posed for a picture around 1910. Courtesy Benzie Area Historical Museum.

Out of the county's total of 222, 483 acres, less than 10 percent (19,844 acres) are now in agriculture, according to the Michigan Agricultural Statistics Service. The number of farms has declined steadily since World War II. There are only one hundred and twenty remaining and only fifty-five report annual sales of more than $10,000 a year, indicating that their owners supplement their income with off-farm jobs. Fruit is the largest crop, with 1,300 acres in tart cherries and 1,190 acres in apples.

Given all of the above, it's paradoxical that farming provided—and to a lesser extent continues to provide—a sense of rural community. To drive the back roads today is to appreciate, even in the face of occasional abandoned barns and farmhouses, that agriculture is still a primary thread in the county's social fabric. That thread is woven tightly in the memories of people like Smeltzer.

"When I was growing up, I knew who lived in 90 percent of the houses," he said. He remembers accompanying his father and an uncle in the early 1920s in a Napoleon truck as they went from farm to farm selling fruit and other produce other farmers did not raise. "If we got there at noon, we always had to stay and eat," he said.

The most successful fruit farms are in the townships of Blaine and Joyfield (where Smeltzer farms) because Lake Michigan moderates the weather. Benzie County farmers were among the first in northwest Michigan to take advantage of the phenomenon.

"For many years, the county led the state in the production of apples," Norman said, "and the first cherry cooperative in northwest Michigan was started by Benzie County farmers."

He said he would be surprised if there are now more than twenty acres of peaches in the county. Peaches were once a major crop. William G. Voorheis demonstrated the possibility of growing them in 1866. He planted hundreds of acres and even developed a variety called the "Frankfort." The

Chicago market was readily accessible by steamship. Peaches had an advantage because the trees produce a crop two or three years after planting, compared to the four to six years it takes for apple and cherry trees to mature. They are, however, more susceptible to frost, which eventually proved to be their undoing.

Other farmers followed Voorheis' example. At one time peaches were such a significant crop that when South Frankfort decided in 1911 to change its name, it chose to call itself Elberta, the name of the most popular variety grown in the area. Peaches were largely abandoned after severe frosts wiped out the orchards several times.

Elberta had a thriving fruit and vegetable processing industry from the early 1900s through the 1950s. At various times, peaches, cherries, and apples, strawberries, raspberries, and plums, as well as onions, celery, and cabbage were prepared for market. One of the more significant processors was the Elberta Packing Co., established in 1936. It was owned by Sam and Max Cohodas, brothers in a prominent Upper Peninsula family which had orchard holdings in the western Lower Peninsula.

Norman of the Extension Service said the decline of agriculture in Benzie County has been part of a national trend.

"When I came in 1974," he said, "the era of the family farm was already passing. When I retire, I doubt if another extension agent will be appointed. When people ask me about agriculture in Benzie County, I tell them about all the new golf courses that have been built.

"Don't laugh. There's not much difference between growing grass for people to walk on and growing grass for cattle to walk on."

A truckload of apples is on its way to market. Fruit has been the most stable crop in Benzie County. Courtesy Robert Kirshner.

Neighboring farmers gathered to pack the apple harvest in barrels, as is shown in this picture taken near Putneys Corners around 1910. Courtesy Benzie Area Historical Museum.

Picking strawberries by hand was backbreaking work.

Courtesy Benzie County Historical Museum.

Before tractors came into general use, scenes of farmers stacking straw on a horse-drawn wagon were common. Courtesy Robert L. McCall.

The Pet-Ritz Co. had about a hundred employees at one time making cherry pies and other products. The plant closed about ten years ago, and the operation was moved to St. Louis. Courtesy Benzie Area Historical Museum.

The third automobile in Benzie County, a Model T Ford shown here in 1913, was owned by James Rice. Courtesy James Rice Family.

In the early 1900s, people like Alma Covey treated a good cow as if it was almost a member of the family. Norman Covey Collection.

CHAPTER 7 RESORTS AND TOURISM

"Frankfort has now a respectable number of tourists who have left the heated cities and are enjoying the health-giving air and lake breezes. The mineral springs and baths are affecting some cures that, if heralded abroad, would soon cause an influx of invalids which would necessitate the building of larger hotels than our village now contains."

The Benzie Banner, July 19, 1888

Beginning with the first settlers, the people of Frankfort knew they were in a special place.

In the summer, there were the wide Lake Michigan beaches for swimming and sunset watching, a fisherman's paradise of inland lakes and streams, pleasantly warm days and cool nights. Winter was another matter, of course, but in those days people thought of it as a season only to be suffered until the daffodils bloomed.

A few travelers on excursion boats from Chicago would visit, but for the most part they were thought of as curiosities, a distraction from the serious work of shipping lumber, smelting ore, and commercial fishing. With the coming of the Ann Arbor railroad in 1892, however, local attitudes began to change. Passenger trains linked Frankfort to the network of rails that ran not only from Chicago, but also from such cities to the east as Detroit, Toledo, and Cleveland from which there had been virtually no access before. Cross-lake car ferries operated by the railroads gave easy access to Milwaukee and other cities on the western shore of Lake Michigan.

People began thinking of tourism in terms of its economic potential, and before long they were even describing it as an industry. Little did they know that someday it would become the dominant industry. As other

A vacation was sometimes a formal affair for families that gathered on the Lake Michigan beach north of Frankfort early in the century. Courtesy Benzie Area Historical Museum.

industries have come and gone—lumbering, the cross-lake car ferries, various manufacturing enterprises—tourism has endured. It is now the mainstay of the economy.

The railroad changed perceptions of Frankfort and Benzie County.

"Frankfort's people speak of their sunsets as though the heavens were especially gracious to this little corner of God's country," the railroad said in a brochure entitled *Away from the Workaday World—An Honest Effort to Picture the Charms of Frankfort.* The railroad's faith in the area's vacation potential went well beyond printing a few brochures. It built one of the finest hotels in the Midwest.

The Ann Arbor Railroad established a depot in Frankfort and built the Royale Frontenac Hotel in 1900 to attract tourists to the area. The hotel burned in1912. Courtesy Charles Webb Fairchild Family.

Construction of the Royale Frontenac Hotel began in 1900, and it was opened the following summer. It had three stories with 250 rooms and verandahs on all sides. The same contractor who built the Grand Hotel on Mackinac Island built the Royale Frontenac. A large, wooded hill was leveled for the building site at the mouth of Betsie Bay. It was near the place where Fr. Marquette, the famous French missionary and explorer, was buried in 1675. The name of the hotel was that of a governor of Quebec who supported Marquette's adventures.

With the Frontenac, vacationers had more to do than watch the sunsets and delight in the cool lake breezes. There was swimming, boating, and horseback riding. The railroad built a nine-hole golf course at the east end of Frankfort. Piping water from Frankfort's mineral springs well to the hotel's bathhouse provided mineral baths, a health fetish of the time. The well, which has been a village landmark since it was drilled in 1881, is rich in sulfates. The present American Legion was originally the bathhouse. The hotel had a ballroom and a game room that included slot machines. Help had to be brought in to supplement the local labor pool, so black students from Fisk College in Tennessee were hired each summer. In the beginning, the hotel was profitable, but when it closed following in 1911 season, there were reports that it was losing money.

On the night of January 12, 1912, there had been a Frankfort High School girls' basketball game, with a dance afterward at the Eagle's Hall. When the fire alarm sounded around midnight, most people had gone to bed. Word spread quickly. The Frontenac was burning. People dressed and hurried to the scene. Bill Rathburn, manager of the hotel's game room, was among the first to arrive and although the fire was rapidly growing beyond control, he was able to rescue his slot machines. Others followed. With flames licking their heels, they took anything they could carry: lamps, mirrors, chairs, kitchen utensils, even beds. The sacking ended as the wooden hotel burned to its foundations. There were inquiries in the days that followed and the threat of prosecutions.

Sensing that Benzie County officials were not anxious to arrest local citizens, the railroad sent in its own detectives. A stanza of a poem the sheriff later wrote, seems to confirm the railroad's suspicion:

They said they'd prosecute the thieves
And went looking up the names.
They marched down through our little town
Like Frank and Jessie James.
They took them from the business places
They took them from the slums
They took a lot of blooded stock
And also several bums.

From the hills above Frankfort, the Royale Frontenac was a commanding presence at the mouth of Betsie Bay. Although it was in business for only a decade, it ushered in a new era of tourism for the area. Courtesy Benzie Area Historical Museum.

The defendants, bum and blooded alike, were offered a deal. If they would return the stolen items, the Justice of the Peace said, felony charges would not be filed. On the appointed day, an embarrassed lot of looters appeared in court to return the goods. The Justice fined each of them $9.10. What may have been a much greater crime—the fire itself—was never solved, despite a widespread belief that it was arson.

There was talk of rebuilding, but it was not to happen. The property sat vacant decade after passing decade. In the early 1950s, the Ann Arbor abandoned its train service to Frankfort, although it still ran into Elberta to service the car ferries. The railroad held onto the property until 1962, when it finally offered to sell it to the city for $10,000. The city didn't have the money, so area businessmen and the Chamber of Commerce bought the property on the condition that it be used for commercial purposes, specifically for a bowling alley, dining facilities and cocktail lounge. A restaurant and bowling alley called—what else?—the Frontenac was opened on the site in 1967. The business closed in 1979. It reopened in 1982 as the Harbor Lights Restaurant and in 1986, a dozen condominiums and eighteen motel rooms were also built on the site. Since then, it has become the Harbor Lights Motel and Condominiums with a hundred rooms, including twenty-six condominiums.

During the Royale Frontenac's short reign as the "pride of Frankfort," it attracted many Jewish patrons from throughout the Midwest. After the hotel burned, they kept coming, and it became commonplace for Frankfort families to rent out their homes to Jewish families. Local residents would then stay in cottages they built facing the alleys at the back of their property. Many of the cottages remain to this day.

"They would return year after year and stay at the same house," said a longtime Frankfort resident. "We were glad to have them, but we could never quite understand why none of them ever just bought a house here."

The practice continued until World War II. After the war, many gravitated to Charlevoix, where an active Jewish vacation community was developing. Another factor was that American's travel habits were changing. Summer-long vacations, with the mother and children staying for weeks on end while the father traveled back and forth from the city on weekends, became the exception, rather than the norm. The automobile began to replace the train, giving people greater flexibility in their choices. And air conditioning made summer more bearable in places lacking cooling lake breezes.

Besides the Frontenac, Frankfort had several other hotels at the turn of the century that mainly served salesmen, lumbermen, and the occasional vacationer. The first, built in 1867, was the Frankfort House. Opened a short time later were the Hotel Koch and the Park Hotel. The Frankfort House later became the Yeazel, which burned in 1926. It was rebuilt and is still operating as the Hotel Frankfort, one of the finest small hotels in northern Michigan. (The present owners also own the Brookside Inn in Beulah.)

A lazy Sunday afternoon, a pleasant stream, and a picnic to follow. Such pleasantries were part of a family outing around 1900. They still are, but bonnets for the women and straw hats for the men have gone out of fashion. Courtesy Frances P. Larson.

Tourism was dealt a near fatal blow nationally during the Great Depression. Frankfort was hit particularly hard because of its isolation. The excursion boats from Chicago cut back on their schedules and then all but stopped running. The railroad trimmed back on passenger service. Aggravating Benzie County's plight was its rudimentary road system. The only was to reach Frankfort easily by car, for instance, was from the north or south. Community leaders, led by Arthur Peterson, the editor of the *Benzie County Patriot,* lobbied successfully for an east-west connection. The unpaved road running east from Frankfort was upgraded to become Michigan 115. The first section, from Frankfort to Benzonia where it connected with U.S. 31, was completed in 1934. It was later extended southeast to Cadillac and beyond, opening Frankfort to the Detroit area. Still recovery was slow until after World War II.

The postwar years ushered in a gradual recovery. The rental cottages on Lake Michigan, Crystal Lake, and elsewhere in the county again were filled in the summers. As before, however, few people saw the likelihood of attracting visitors during the winter. Ward Creech, a skiing enthusiast and the principal of Benzonia High School, did not have tourism in mind when he built a tow line in his back yard, but his enthusiasm for the emerging sport would have positive consequences for the county. His makeshift ski run was soon overrun by demand and so, in 1955, he and others opened the Buck Hills community skiing area, west of Thompsonville. It was the beginning of what would become Crystal Mountain Resort, which is today the single largest employer in the county, with 350 employees during peak seasons.

A group of investors, many of whom had cottages on Crystal Lake, bought Buck Hills in 1960. The principal investor was Ed Abbey, a Toledo automobile broker and real estate investor. The Buck Hills warming hut was replaced by a lodge, with rooms, a restaurant, and a cocktail lounge called Club 96 because that was the number of investors involved. A chair lift was imported from Germany. For the next five years or so, it operated as a sort of down-home resort where the rates were lower than at other resorts in northern Michigan, but where the ambiance was more family oriented and friendlier than elsewhere.

George Petritz, a colorful Frankfort businessman, acquired the resort in 1966. Under his leadership it has become one of the region's major resorts. He came to the venture in a roundabout way. Raised in Rockford, Illinois, Petritz went on to study business administration at Notre Dame and the

The 250-room Royale Frontenac was a backdrop for activities on Betsie Bay, whether it was men from the U.S. Life Saving Service practicing righting a capsized rescue boat or the arrival of the 267-ton Richard Motl schooner from Chicago. Courtesy of Benzie Shores District Library and the Charles Webb Fairchild Family.

The Park Hotel was one of Frankfort's first, opening several years after the end of the Civil War. Courtesy Robert L. McCall.

The Marine Ball Room near Frankfort was a local hotspot in the 1920s and 1930s. Courtesy Robert L. McCall.

University of Marquette. Prior to the war, he worked as sales manager of a manufacturer of playground, gymnasium, and swimming pool equipment. During the war, he was a PT boat commander and was captured by the Japanese, an experience for which he was awarded the Navy Cross. After the war, he worked for IBM for several years but then decided he was a small town boy at heart.

Members of the Congregational Summer Assembly strolled down Frankfort's Main Street in 1906 while they waited for a carriage to come and take them to the assembly grounds on Crystal Lake. Courtesy Congregational Summer Assembly.

"Literally, the first day I saw Crystal Lake, I knew 'that's it,'" he told an interviewer. "It's been hard to get me out of Benzie County ever since . . ."

He became involved in the business of the family of his wife, Althea. Her family had started the Cherry Hut restaurant in Beulah in the 1920s. In 1946 they decided that the pies that had become so popular at the restaurant could be manufactured in quantity and frozen for sale nationally. The business was sold to Pet Milk in 1955. Petritz stayed on with the new owners for a couple of years, but left when it became clear he would have to leave the area. He had dabbled in other ventures before the Crystal Mountain opportunity arose.

"That's been my main thrust ever since," he said.

Today, Crystal Mountain is a 1,500-acre year-round resort, with lodging for more than 900 people. There are twenty-five downhill ski slopes, thirty kilometers of groomed cross country ski trails, twenty-seven holes of golf, indoor and outdoor pools, tennis, and mountain biking. There is a 175-seat restaurant and conference facilities. In the spring of 1997 the resort was undergoing a major expansion, with the addition of nine holes of golf and a new hotel complex.

While Crystal Mountain may have led the way, the rest of the county has not been far behind.

A major boom to tourism came in 1972 when the 71,000-acre Sleeping Bear Dunes National Lakeshore was established. The southern half of the national park is in Benzie County, where there are some of the most spectacular dunes—some rising 450 feet—on Lake Michigan. It gets nearly a million and a half visitors a year.

Lake Michigan defines the western end of the county, attracting not only beachcombers but also boaters and fishermen. There are four marinas on Betsie Bay. Nearly twenty charter fishing boats are moored on the bay to take people fishing for salmon and lake trout. For those seeking gentler waters, the county has fifty-five inland lakes, ranging in size from Crystal Lake down to those so small they constitute secret fishing holes for the few anglers who have sought them out. There are two major rivers, the Betsie and the Platte for fly-fishing, as well as a number of secondary streams.

Not all of Benzie County's early-day tourists came by train. Luxury lake steamers like the *Puritan* and the *Missouri* brought people from Chicago and Milwaukee. Courtesy Congregational Summer Assembly.

The Buck Hills community ski area was purchased by investors in 1966 and renamed Crystal Mountain resort. By 1970, with its new lodge, it had a state-wide reputation as a family oriented resort. Courtesy Crystal Mountain Resort.

Benzie County is becoming a golfer's mecca. Besides Crystal Mountain, there are four other public courses—the Frankfort Golf Club in Frankfort, Pinecroft Golf Plantation and Crystal Lake Golf Club at Beulah, and Mistwood Golf Course at Lake Ann.

When civic boosters spoke of tourism in the 1900s as an industry, they may have been stretching its importance. Today there can be no doubt as to its influence, and indications are that it will become even more significant in the future. More than half the 6,000 jobs in the county are dependent on tourism. Other counties in northwest Michigan have been overwhelmed by commercial development that accompanies a tourism boom. Benzie County has retained its original charm. There are still unsullied beaches to walk, miles of streams to wade and lonely country roads that meander through orchards.

And in the evening, the sun sets in the same spectacular way it has for eons. If you listen carefully, the Indians told the early settlers, you may hear it sizzle as it settles under the Lake Michigan horizon.

Before the Buck Hills community ski facility was established, skiing was a rag-tag recreation in Benzie County. Buck Hills, with minimal amenities, later developed into Crystal Mountain Resort. The resort has expanded several times and now has a modern lodge with an indoor swimming pool. The slopes, both downhill and cross-country, are groomed daily. The resort caters to golfers in the summer. Courtesy Frances P. Larson and Crystal Mountain Resort.

CHAPTER 8 FISHING: COMMERCIAL AND SPORTS

"The perfectly astounding feature of the debacle was that despite the Coast Guard warning . . . fishermen kept heading for the lake for more fishing, much like lemming in the Scandinavian countries on their periodical suicide missions."

The Benzie County Patriot, Sept. 28, 1967

It wasn't as if fishermen hadn't been warned.

"Caution, Please!" the headline in Frankfort's weekly newspaper pleaded the week before the September 1967 storm in which seven men drowned and scores of boats were battered to pieces on the beach around Point Betsie, north of Frankfort.

"Attempting to go out into Lake Michigan when the seas are running too high has caused more than one boat to sink," said the story, which, in retrospect, seems a prelude to the tragic storm. "Inadequate boating equipment such as 10-foot prams with 1 1/2-horsepower motors, canoes, rubber dinghies, etc., have also caused their share of headaches."

Hundreds of fishermen failed to heed the warning, throwing caution literally to the wind during the first Coho salmon run on Lake Michigan. The fish were huge and easy to catch. For anglers whose biggest thrill before had been hooking a four-pound bass, the fifteen- and twenty-pound salmon were mesmerizing. Fishermen came from throughout the Midwest, sometimes driving all night and hauling little boats that would be better suited for farm ponds.

Artist Zoltan L. Sepeshy (1898–1974), a summer resident of Frankfort, was captivated by the commercial fishing docks. In a series of paintings, he strove to relate the scene for posterity. In this painting, entitled "Olsen's Men," he put Ole Olsen, the man with a white shirt and suspenders, in the center working alongside his men. The Pennsylvania Academy of the Fine Arts.

It's not as if the passions of fishing were something new for Benzie County. Fishing had run in the county's lifeblood since the earliest settlers set gill nets for lake trout and whitefish, establishing the county's oldest business. With the proximity of Lake Michigan and more than fifty inland lakes and several trout streams, the county had long had a reputation among the rod-and-reel set as a fisherman's paradise.

An arsenal of fishing gear (rods and reels, downriggers, and catch nets) clutters the back of charter fishing boats on Betsie Bay.
Photo by Thomas BeVier.

George Richey, a veteran Benzie County fishing guide, spoke from experience when he said, "You can spend a lifetime fishing in Benzie County." And he knows as well as anyone how the salmon revolutionized that paradise.

"They changed the economy," he said. "My brother Dave (now the outdoors editor for *The Detroit News*) and I started guiding in 1968. We were the first to catch them on a fly rod. They put Honor (on the Platte River, where the fish return to spawn) on the map. Before we knew it, Frankfort had a hundred charter boats."

Richey's life revolves around fishing. To hear him describe a typical year of fishing is to appreciate how rich a resource Benzie County has.

"In the winter, there's great ice fishing for perch and lake trout on Crystal Lake and for pike and bluegills on almost all the inland lakes. As spring breaks, there's trolling for brown trout on the big lake in late May. The steelhead start coming up the Platte and the Betsie late in February and continue through April of mid-May. In the summer, Herring Lake is good for walleye. In June, the Chinook salmon (another species that were later introduced) start showing up."

When the big fish aren't running, he's apt to be found fishing for bluegills on such lakes as Glovers, Otter, Bass, Sanford, and both Upper and Lower Herring. Brundage Creek is his favorite brook trout stream.

Nothing in his angling experience prepared him, or anybody else for that matter, for the salmon frenzy in 1967. "It was crazy," he said.

The out-of-town fishermen all but commandeered Frankfort. They fought among themselves for turns at the town's few launch ramps. The placid residential neighborhoods were overrun by caravans of fishermen looking for places to park. Tents were pitched on schoolhouse lawns. Parking lots were filled with campers. Sporting goods stores, groceries and party stores were stripped of merchandise.

John Clevinger of the state Department of Natural Resources is an overseer at the department's Platte River Anadromous Fish Hatchery near Honor, where salmon are raised for stocking in Lake Michigan and Lake Huron. Photo by Thomas BeVier.

State Department of Natural Resources had planted the Coho in Michigan rivers in the hope that their voracious appetites would tame the lake's alewife population. The alewife is an Atlantic Ocean species that migrated into the Great Lakes through the St. Lawrence Seaway. With no predators to control them the alewives had multiplied out of control. During a die-off each spring, the stench of their rotting bodies was damnation for beaches. Not only did the salmon gobble up the alewives, they also established a brand new fishery.

In recent years, the salmon population, under stress of fishing and disease, has fallen off, but in September 1967 they were intoxicatingly plentiful.

"Most people at one time or another have probably wondered what northern California and the Klondike were like during the Gold Rush days," said the lead paragraph of a September 7, 1967, story in the *Benzie County Patriot.* "During the past weekend, they could have witnessed a reenactment of that era by visiting Manistee, Frankfort, or the mouth of the Platte River. It wasn't gold that called the prospectors to the area but Coho salmon that are presently running in Lake Michigan in astounding numbers and sizes."

When the storm hit the following week, fishermen continued launching their boats. At Frankfort, in the lee of Point Betsie, the conditions did not appear all that dangerous from the shore, but beyond the point there were gale-force winds and twenty-five-foot waves. The next edition of the paper carried a picture of scores of boats that smashed up on the beach. DUNKIRK IN REVERSE! shouted the caption accompanying the photograph.

"As had been feared by local residents since the fun began a month ago, the Coho salmon, like the Lorelei at the Rhine, finally lured a number of fishermen to their deaths last Saturday," the paper reported. "Fishermen who were clinging to boat cushions, empty gas cans, and portions of boats were helped ashore and rushed to the local hospital . . . Shortly after 2:30 p.m., the bodies began to wash up . . . Many of the fishermen caught in high seas had never before been on Lake Michigan and did not realize how vicious this large body of water can become in a short time . . .

None of the seven who died was a local resident. Shaken, the fishermen quickly left. "Frankfort is a wonderful town," said a Grand Rapids man who had clung to a gas can for two and a half hours after his boat capsized. "The people have been most hospitable and helpful, and I hope I never see it again."

Before the salmon were planted, the Lake Michigan fishery had deteriorated from excess harvesting by commercial fishermen and an infestation of lamprey, another ocean species that made its way into the lakes through the Seaway. The parasitic, eel-like lamprey devastated lake trout and whitefish populations. Another factor was that state and federal politicians were bent on transforming the lakes from a commercial to a sports fishery, as towns became increasingly tourist-oriented. Sleek charter boats, with their arsenals of rods and downriggers, were to replace the workhorse fishing tugs that had lined the Frankfort shoreline for so many decades.

"I can remember one of my father's boats coming in after catching just one whitefish," said Joan Carlson, the daughter of Ole Olsen, a well-known fisherman whose Norwegian immigrant father had started fishing with a sailboat in the 1880s. "He just shut it down." Her brother, Edward "Bud" Olsen, fished for several more years. The family's last boat, the *Buddy O,* is now part of a fishing museum in Two Rivers, Wisconsin.

She remembers the sound of the diesel engines as the boats left the harbor before dawn to fish around the Manitou Islands, the lusty taunts of men when they returned, the haggling between her father and resort owners over the price of fish. Her cousin, Dr. William R. Olsen, a retired surgeon, also grew up around the docks. His memories are of cleaning fish and putting them on ice, cranking nets onto huge reels to dry, delivering fish on his bicycle.

He can still recall the names of those who had boats. Starting at the Coast Guard station at the harbor entrance, he started naming them. "There was Captain Waters—"Boogie," he was called—and then Anderson Brothers. Next were Rodal and the Luedtke Engineering docks. Hanrath was next and then Olsen. I think Chapin was next and, finally, Groesser. That's most of them." Many of the families had more than one boat; Dr. Olsen said there were twenty-two boats at the docks when he was in high school. A Detroit area artist, Zoltan L. Sepeshy (1898–1974), who spent summers at Frankfort, painted pictures of the fishermen. Much of his work is now at the Pennsylvania Academy of Fine Arts in Philadelphia. One of the paintings, *Olsens' Men,* shows Ole Olsen working alongside his employees.

The boats worked even in the winter when Lake Michigan was treacherous with ice. In *Memos of Betsie Bay,* Charles M. Anderson, who was from a well-known fishing family, related in a matter-of-fact way what that was like. "It would be snowing and cold," he wrote. "We would set our nets, then go into South Manitou harbor for the balance of the night. We would

Ole Olsen, patriarch of a Betsie Bay commercial fishing family, repairs his gill nets in 1959. Courtesy Joan O. Carlson.

try and sleep in a net box that was empty of nets. We would pull anchor before daylight and head out to the nets that were set at midnight to fill them for the day's catch."

Sometimes boats did not survive cold, snowy nights.

Betsie Bay was packed with ice in March 1934 when the *Jean R.* set out with three other tugs to tend nets they had set earlier. A heavy snowstorm, however, soon forced them to turn back. Three boats made it back, although not without damage. The *Jean R.* was trapped in the ice just outside the harbor. People bundled against the weather gathered on shore to watch as waves threatened to smash her against the north breakwall. There was a dramatic moment when it appeared certain that the boat would sink with its four-man crew aboard, but the Coast Guard managed to secure a line between the tug and the lighthouse at the tip of the breakwall. The crew climbed hand-over-hand from the boat to safety. As the last man made it, a wave picked the boat up and dashed it against the concrete, sinking it. It was raised in the summer and put back in service the next fall.

When the logging boom was coming to an end in 1936, Honor pharmacist Wesley B. Covey began stocking fishing tackle as the number of visiting anglers increased. Norman Covey Collection.

The charter boats that replaced the fishing fleet are a gentler breed, more timid about going out in bad weather. Their clientele, after all, are sportsmen in pursuit of a good time, and there's nothing like a gale to spoil the fun and cause a doubling of liability premiums in the bargain. One problem they share is that sometimes there aren't enough fish. Salmon stocks, for instance, have declined and with them also the number of charter boats. There are now only fifteen moored in Betsie Bay, compared to the hundred at the offset.

As some fishermen see it—at least those who choose to write about it— fishing is more than the pursuit of game. There's also the philosophical aspect. Benzie County has attracted its share of angling philosophers. You see them standing thigh deep in rushing streams, contemplating which fly to try next to tempt the elusive trout. And one can only marvel at the patience of the bass fishermen who cast their weekends away on any number of Benzie County lakes in the summertime. L. F. Brown, a writer for *The Amateur Sportsman* in the early 1900s was that sort. He lived in New York City and season after season he came to Benzie County for what he considered some of the best fishing in America. His flowery prose, however overwrought and corny in its enthusiasms by contemporary standards, still resonates, suggesting that Benzie County is as good a place as any to wet a line.

"WANTED," he wrote at the beginning of an article in 1904. "Good angling, varied but all right at hand, a good country house or hotel in the middle of the angling region. There must be a lovely trout stream for fly casting, one or more lakes for bass, another for pickerel and muskalongs (muskellunges) . . . Exacting requirements, yet Platte fills them."

For what he found in northern Michigan, he would ride for two days on a train. And then, in print, he would brag a bit and reflect a lot.

Sometimes fish stories are true, as a picture of a Lake Trout caught in the 1940s proves. Courtesy the Hanrath family.

Fishing like this is a thing of the past. Courtesy Benzie Area Historical Museum.

The *Sea Bird* gill net fishing boat was one of the sleekest craft on Betsie Bay. Courtesy Charles Webb Fairchild Family.

As for bragging: "In one hour, as we used lines with double hooks, the catch of perch was made as shown in the illustration herewith, and that afternoon 250 yellow perch went 10 miles to the 60 (railroad) shopmen at Frankfort." (The railroad workers had asked Brown's party to catch a few for them.)

The Platte River has always provided fishermen with a "blessed escape." Courtesy Lois Bender.

A hawk killing a mocking bird angered him. "And yet what right had I to rail at that hawk?" he wrote. "It was the play of the survival of the fittest. Here was I with a creel half full of brook trout that I had killed. What better was the angler than the hawk?"

He wrote of experiencing "renewed courage and hope" and of "restorations of health." Sitting at his Underwood back in New York, writing an article entitled *Frankfort Lake Region Angling Memories,* his reverie slipped all bounds.

"It was a blessed escape," he wrote. The testimonial serves to this day.

CHAPTER 9 THE PRESENT AND A GLIMPSE BEYOND

"The world we have lost might be a nice place to visit, but we would not want to live there. The present may be disturbing and the future may be in the highest degree ominous, but nobody gains anything by seeing in the irrecoverable past a charm and comfort which it did not have."

Bruce Catton, *Waiting for the Morning Train*

Nearly one hundred and fifty years ago, Joseph Oliver, a trapper and fisherman, came to the shores of Betsie Bay with his Indian wife. He liked what he saw. He built a cabin, becoming the first settler in what was to become Benzie County. Others soon followed, and Oliver was a leader in the new community. In his later years, he was known as the "grand old man of Gilmore," the name of the township he helped organize.

It may be an embellishment to suggest that the view of Betsie Bay sustained him through difficult times, although he doubtless appreciated natural beauty; he saw to the planting of one hundred and five maple trees to provide shade at the Gilmore Township Cemetery, where he was later buried. But it is certainly not an exaggeration to say that the view provided an accurate assessment of how history was advancing.

The same can be said about Betsie Bay to this very day. Its view is still sustaining, and the changes that have occurred there suggest what the future holds for Frankfort and Benzie County. Cathy Carter, director of Benzie Shores District Library, said as much when she described her workaday surroundings.

"I don't know of a library anywhere else that has sailboats moored beside its lawn," she said, commending the view of Frankfort's Municipal Marina through the library's expansive windows. "I never get tired of looking at it."

Despite growth and development, there is still no problem finding a quiet place to be by yourself, as Mrs. Henry Banister did around 1905 on a bluff overlooking the beach north of Frankfort. Courtesy the Charles Webb Fairchild family.

The Benzie Shores District Library sets the tone for a rejuvenated Betsie Bay waterfront. Courtesy Betsie Bay District Library.

The $411,000 library, a book browser's delight with its airy spaciousness, was opened in 1994. It exemplifies not only a new look for the bay but also a new outlook for Frankfort and Benzie County. It and other developments are part of a renaissance to take advantage of an altered economy, an economy that depends on tourism and retirees.

Visitors stroll the Frankfort shoreline on brick paths, graced with flower gardens and neatly kept lawns. On the main street, old stores have been spruced up to reflect their Victorian era heritage and new ones have been opened to cater to tourists.

"The town has transformed itself," said Robert C. Foster, president and chief executive officer of West Michigan National Bank & Trust. "It's been good for the economy."

He points out that with improvements in communication and the advent of computers, "small towns no longer need to be left out." Three years ago, for instance, most of Benzie County depended on dial telephones. The system is now digitized. "We get inquiries from people who want to set up small shops here," he said. Another improvement in the offing is improved airport facilities. Foster is chairman of the Frankfort City-County Airport Authority, which is overseeing a $1.8 million improvement project that includes lengthening and widening the runway, providing paved automobile and aircraft parking and installing improved lighting. There are long range plans to build a terminal and to provide additional taxi ways and parking.

For Erich Luedtke, whose family has operated Luedtke Engineering Co. on the Frankfort waterfront since 1930, the transformation is particularly dramatic. "In the 1950s, the bay was so filthy you wouldn't dare swim in it," he said. He recalls a waterfront given over to commercial fishing vessels and industrial users. Across the bay in Elberta was the Ann Arbor Railroad cross-lake car ferry service. Not much attention was given to neatness.

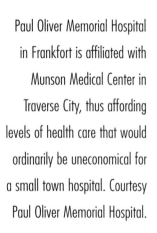

Paul Oliver Memorial Hospital in Frankfort is affiliated with Munson Medical Center in Traverse City, thus affording levels of health care that would ordinarily be uneconomical for a small town hospital. Courtesy Paul Oliver Memorial Hospital.

"The whole character of the area is changing," said Luedtke, whose company does marine contracting throughout the Great Lakes. "A lot of people are moving up. We were at the bottom (economically) fifteen years ago. The summer people have been a blessing. They have enabled the community to progress. If it wasn't for them, we wouldn't have our hospital or our library."

Few towns of Frankfort's size (population 1,650) are fortunate enough to have a facility like Paul Oliver Memorial Hospital. The forty-eight-bed facility—forty for long-term care patients—provides local health care access. It is part of the Munson Healthcare System, which manages several small hospitals in northwest Michigan and provides direct access to the physicians and staff of Munson Medical Center, the regional care facility in Traverse City. On site Paul Oliver has twenty-four-hour urgent care, long-term care, respite care and acute care. It has a laboratory, x-ray, mammography, ultrasound, physical and respiratory therapy, cardiac rehabilitation, and a number of other specialty services.

The hospital is a prime example of an institution keeping pace with the times. It traces its origin to the Haldeman Hospital for maternity patients, which was opened in a converted residence in 1931 and was operated by Adele Oliver R.N. until 1937. It was replaced by Anna Markham Memorial Hospital, which was closed in 1951 when Paul Oliver Memorial Hospital was opened. It is named after a Chicago physician who was a summer resident in the area for many years and provided financial support. It affiliated with Munson in 1987 and in 1995 a $2.5 million renovation and expansion was completed.

As the hospital was helped by a newcomer to the area so were other projects. The library received a large grant from the Seabury Foundation, named after a Chicago family that has vacationed in the area for generations.

Jacobson Marina—one of four marinas on Betsie Bay—was made possible by private investors, who have vacation homes on Crystal Lake.

"For its size, it's as nice a facility as you'll find," said Art Moseler, manager of the Jacobson Marina. "When I was growing up, this was a dirty, grubby area. In my younger days, pleasure boats were few and far between. We had the car ferries and the harbor had a reputation of being for commercial boats."

More than half the jobs in the county are directly dependent on tourism and that appears to be the wave of the future, although there are indications that the economic base may become more diversified. A number of small manufacturers have built facilities and existing ones are expanding. In mid–1997, for instance, Frankfort Manufacturing began construction of a new factory, which will more than double its capacity. The company, which manufactures fasteners such as screws, has been a Frankfort mainstay for nearly fifty years.

While change is perhaps most obvious in Frankfort, it also applies to most of the rest of the county.

The county's many lakes are ringed with new homes and the old ones have been remodeled. Several condominium developments have sprung up in recent years. Benzonia has been lovingly maintained to reflect its historical roots as the county's first settlement as a Congregational Church colony. Beulah, at its cozy setting at the eastern end of Crystal Lake, retains the same charm it had when it became the first town in the county to concentrate on tourism. Dusty, unkept patches in the middle of the small towns, like Lake Ann and Honor, have been made into parks. Thompsonville, which almost became a ghost town, is being revived by the ongoing development of nearby Crystal Mountain resort.

Few towns have suffered as great an economic reverse as Elberta and survived. When the car ferry service was terminated in 1982, Elberta's economy was devastated. Things are about to change. In 1997, the village purchased from the Michigan Department of Transportation the 21.5 acres on its waterfront that Ann Arbor Railroad had used for its operations. Plans are already underway for a residential, commercial, and recreational development. "That property is the key to our future," said Greg Jenks, the village president.

A lot has changed in downtown Frankfort since this picture of Main Street was taken in 1940. Specialized shops that cater to tourists have been added, an indication of a changing economy. Courtesy Robert L. McCall.

Newly planted trees, benches for strollers to rest and stores interspersed with park-like open spaces give it a relaxed air. Photo by Thomas BeVier.

Unlike other places in northwest Michigan, which has enjoyed a tourist boom in the last twenty years, Benzie County has not been overwhelmed by it. There is concern, however, about repeating mistakes that were made in Grand Traverse County to the north, which is struggling with traffic problems and urban sprawl. Benzie County's master plan is being updated. The Citizens Advisory Committee, formed initially in a successful effort to save an early-day schoolhouse and keep a fast food restaurant from being built on the site, has broadened its objectives and is working closely with local government.

The Point Betsie Lighthouse has been a landmark since the first settlers came to Benzie County. Courtesy Robert L. McCall.

"We've still got time to adjust and do things right to handle growth," said Robert McNabb, president of the Frankfort Chamber of Commerce and chairman of the city planning commission. "We're getting our act together."

Bibliography

Anderson, Charles M. *Memos of Betsie Bay, A History of Frankfort,* 1988.

Bellak, Theodore. *Memoirs of Gliding and Soaring,* Pine Hill Press, 1995.

Blacklock, Allen B. *History of Elberta.*

Case, Leonard. *Benzie County: A Bicentennial Reader,* 1976.

Catton, Bruce. *Waiting for the Morning Train,* Wayne State University Press, 1987.

Catton. Michigan: *A History, W. W. Norton & Co.,* 1976.

Dunbar, Willis F. *Michigan: A History of the Woverine State,* William B. Eerdmann Publishing Co., 1965. (Revised in 1980 by George S. May.)

Frederickson, Arthur C. and Lucy F. *Pictorial History of the C & O Train and Auto Ferries,* Lakeside Printing Co., 1955.

Frederickson. *Early History of the Ann Arbor Carferries,* Patriot Publishing Co., 1949.

Frederickson. *Later History of Ann Arbor Carferries,* 1951.

Havighurst, Walter. *The Long Ships Passing, the story of the Great Lakes,* Macmillan Company, 1942.

Hensel, Dorothy B. *Church of the Wilderness,* Benzie Area Historical Society, 1987.

Howard, John H. *The Story of Frankfort,* Published by Frankfort City Council, 1930.

Howard, *A History of Herring Lake.*

Overlease, William and Edith. *Daylight in the Swamp,* BaySide Printing, 1996.

Sandman, Pete. *Views from God's Country,* Benzie County Record Patriot, 1981.

Stebbins, Catherine L. *Here I Shall Finish My Voyage,* Solle's Press of Omena, 1960.

Wakefield, Larry. *Ghost Towns of Michigan,* Northmont Publishing, 1994.

Wakefield, Larry. *Ghost Towns of Michigan, Volume II,* Thunder Bay Press, 1995.

Index

Author Profile

Photo by John Robert Williams

What began as a six-month assignment to cover northern Michigan for a major Detroit daily newspaper has developed into a lasting commitment to the area for Thomas BeVier. For fifteen years, he has written about the region's politics and peccadilloes and about the special appeal of its people and its landscape.

Most recently, he was the northern Michigan correspondent for The Detroit News. Previously, he worked for The Detroit Free Press. He is a former Journalism Fellow at the University of Michigan.

He lives in Traverse City, Michigan, near the shore of Lake Michigan, with his wife, Meredith, and two Brittany Spaniels. He has five grown children and five grandchildren.